D0079258

Bibliographic Access to Medieval and Renaissance Manuscripts: A Survey of Computerized Data Bases and Information Services

Bibliographic Access to Medieval and Renaissance Manuscripts: A Survey of Computerized Data Bases and Information Services

Wesley M. Stevens
Editor

The Haworth Press, Inc.
New York • London

Bibliographic Access to Medieval and Renaissance Manuscripts: A Survey of Computerized Data Bases and Information Services has also been published as *Primary Sources & Original Works*, Volume 1, Numbers 3/4 1991.

The Haworth Press, Inc., 10 Alice Street, Binghamton, NY 13904-1580 USA

Library of Congress Cataloging-in-Publication Data

Bibliographic access to medieval and renaissance manuscripts : a survey of computerized data bases and information services / Wesley M. Stevens, editor.
     p. cm.
    "Also been published as Primary sources & original works, volume 1, numbers 3/4, 1991" — T.p. verso.
    Includes bibliographical references.
    ISBN 1-56024-224-8 (acid free paper)
    1. Manuscripts, Medieval — Data bases — Directories. 2. Manuscripts, Renaissance — Data bases — Directories. 3. Manuscripts, Medieval — Information services — Directories. 4. Manuscripts, Renaissance — Information services — Directories. I. Stevens, Wesley M.
Z6601.A1B53 1992
025.3'412'0285 — dc20

91-32322
CIP

Bibliographic Access
to Medieval
and Renaissance Manuscripts:
A Survey
of Computerized Data Bases
and Information Services

Bibliographic Access to Medieval and Renaissance Manuscripts: A Survey of Computerized Data Bases and Information Services

CONTENTS

ABOUT THE EDITOR

Dr. Wesley M. Stevens is Professor of History at the University of Winnipeg, Canada. He has been published extensively, and has also served as translator of articles from French and German into English. Professor Stevens is co-director with N. L. Hahn of the Benjamin Catalogue for History of Science and Chairman of the Committee for Manuscript Census Records. He currently serves on the Council of the International Society for the Study of Time, the Corporation Canadienne des Sciences Religieuses, and the Canadian National Committee of the International Union for History and Philosophy of Science.

Preface

When asked by Professor Wesley Stevens to participate in the conferences planned for Hamburg and Munich in 1989 concerning computerized access to medieval and renaissance manuscripts on science and medicine, I had no idea that we would engage in subsequent collaboration in publishing these important papers from the proceedings. As then president of the Association for the Bibliography of History, I had previously committed myself years in advance to organize special sessions on information and historical sciences for the 1990 International Conference on Historical Sciences in Madrid, and in the meantime had accepted an invitation to present another paper at the International Conference on Mediterranean Studies in Murcia, and still another at the Montpellier Computer Conference. This already required two trips to Europe, and neither my stamina or travel funding could sustain a third trip to Germany. My inability to participate personally was regretted because my interest has been longstanding in furthering discussion about the international exchange of information about primary sources — in international conferencing for the promotion of data base development in the Humanities and Social Sciences, membership in the international archives committee of the Society of American Archives, and my recent assumption of editorial responsibilities for *Primary Sources & Original Works*. The latter provided an opportunity to redress my non-participation in the congress for the History of Science and to work with Professor Wesley Stevens in bringing this volume of essays to you.

Once we agreed to publish a series of papers from the conferences devoted to computerized access to medieval and renaissance manuscripts, Professor Stevens asked me to submit the contribution I would have made at the conference had I been able to attend. I had earlier prepared a preliminary paper for the planned conference in

Nijmegen which never materialized; my draft was published (unfortunately without the opportunity to correct a mauled typescript). His invitation provided a chance to revise and update some thoughts about progress in the field and directions for continued development. It came, however, at a time when I was over-committed and had considerable administrative responsibilities to fulfill as a dean and university librarian (which are so inimical to the pursuit of scholarly interests). Nevertheless, this prompt was the stimulus needed to prepare a second essay which represents a stage in continuing development of thoughts about access to medieval primary sources. Indeed, these essays all depict the evolution of thought about modern information technology to assist scholarship based on some of the most difficult of historical sources in Western culture. That scholarship is undergoing significant change; and the technology we contemplate is changing so fast that we are always behind the times. Some would say, our adoption of modern information technology has been really "medieval"!

My reading of these essays has updated my awareness of the problems in thinking about computers and manuscripts, and computerized information sharing through library systems, manual and electronic. We are all caught in this warp, where our sensibilities are teased by possibilities that always seem to evade us for the present. Ours is an intellectual pilgrimage, a travelogue, telling the reader about the difference between where we are and where we want to be, always searching for that distant objective. But rather than crawling or walking, our steps are beginning to pick up pace, with longer strides, and covering greater distance, since the assistance of computers. We are struggling to master them, to use their potential for the maximum benefit, and to envision scholarship once impossible. But in this field, while ourselves being freed from scribal technology, our dependence remains on the scribes of old. Their limitations are still ours, as we return to the sources. The goal, I assume, is to decrease time in our search for their productions, so we can take time in research, content analysis, and the enlargement of the scope of our intellectual embrace.

If these essays broaden the vision, speed project development, encourage communication across departmental and cultural barriers, and urge cooperation, they will be judged successful. Credit for such success goes totally to Professor Wesley Stevens who organized these sessions at the international conference and who brought these contributions to a wider audience through this publication. It has been my pleasure to work with him and to learn from him and our colleagues who have collaborated in this project.

Lawrence J. McCrank, PhD
Editor

Access to Knowledge:
An Introduction

Wesley M. Stevens

Librarians, archivists, and research scholars always have at least two concerns. How may we acquire and preserve an organised body of knowledge? How may we provide that body of knowledge for those who need it? The eleven essays gathered here address these concerns in new ways and with new technologies.

For access to primary sources in manuscript, creators of machine readable manuscript catalogues have proceeded in different ways and at various levels of complexity. In the Benjamin Catalogue for History of Science, Hahn and Stevens intend to meet all the demands of the most systematic cataloguers, and their organisation of expected information allows great detail about the book itself (codicology) and its contents. The contents of a manuscript codex can be quite diverse but usually include separate essays or tracts with different authors, titles, and subject matter. Thus the Benjamin Catalogue uses encoding protocols for 110 fields of data and innumerable sub-types in order to incorporate all data available for a manuscript in quite sophisticated fields without significant limitations. Similarly in the International Computer Catalogue of Medieval Scientific Manuscripts (ICC MSM), Folkerts and Kühne have the same goal of full description, omitting no detail of codicology or contents. This is implemented with an encoding system created by Van Egmond which provides for the physical detail of the writing, materials used, organisation and binding, from which scholars learn to date and place the origin and construction of books. This catalogue is particularly strong in manuscripts containing mathematical texts and has incorporated many records of other scientific manuscripts from the Benjamin Catalogue with which it is compatible. The commendable inclusiveness of the Benjamin Catalogue

1

and the ICC MSM however generates great masses of data, and this produces problems of search and retrieval which they may not yet have solved, though the ICC MSM has made considerable progress with using commercial indices for search and retrieval.

Enlarged memories for new personal computers have finally made such approaches free from the practical problems of sharing time on a larger institutional host computer. For the Hill Monastic Manuscript Library however, Amos accepted the limited capacity of earlier personal computers. He uses a commercial database management system with datafields and retrieval procedures which are strictly limited. Nevertheless within the confines of a data management system which was created for legal and financial files, Amos has defined encoding protocols for data fields which accommodate much sophisticated literary and historical information for the description of both content and codicology of manuscripts. His work thus far has been to prepare a new catalogue of a large collection of manuscripts collected in microfilm at the HMML (Amos, 1988, 1989). It is not clear that his system will be sufficiently flexible for encoding, searching, and retrieving data from many diverse manuscript collections. Touwaide works in a similar manner for analysis of ancient medical texts, wherever found, and he is developing a scholarly workstation with a considerable collection of primary documents in microfilm and with diverse linguistic and historical reference tools. On the other hand Schipke has happily chosen to serve scholarship in many fields of research by providing the incipits of the texts found in manuscripts of German libraries and archives. Use of incipits is a primary way of searching for research materials concerning authors and texts and for identifying differing versions of the same texts.

The Paris computer-assisted catalogue was conceived by Marie-José Beaud and Lucie Fossier at the Institut de recherche et d'histoire des textes and then realised by Guillaumont and Minel in the system called MEDIUM. This menu-driven computer programme allows the scholar in the IRHT to consult descriptive data about manuscripts in a manner which is interactive and rapid. In 1977 this system was intended to include all of the information about each manuscript in the IRHT microfilm collection that would be provided by the best modern printed manuscript catalogues. But in practice it was found that such data had often not been provided by printed catalogues and required original research in itself; furthermore it was time-consuming and thus expensive to encode and verify so much data. There was a decision to reduce expectations somewhat. At present all manuscripts in microfilm of the IRHT are listed in MEDIUM, but the data for each one available by computer are usually quite limited and do not include incipits unless the title of a text has not been identified. MEDIUM is a well-conceived programme which has great promise, and its realisation is far advanced.

Many librarians will turn first to the essay by Dr. Hope Mayo, "MARC Cataloguing for Medieval Manuscripts," and to her second essay, "Standards for Description, Indexing and Retrieval in Computerized Catalogs of Medieval Manuscripts," published earlier (Folkerts and Kühne, 1990). For many years now the U.S. Library of Congress has provided librarians with bibliographic materials for card catalogues and later for on-line catalogues in the format called Machine Readable Cataloguing (MARC). In collaboration with the British National Bibliography, the Library of Congress issued in 1968 a revision of USMARC which has become the standard for library cataloguing in the U.S.A., Great Britain, Canada, and prospectively in the libraries of all English speaking countries. There is also the French MARC, IberoMARC, and an international UNIMARC created to enable record exchange among all MARC systems. UNIMARC may eventually evolve into a more nearly universal format for computer cataloguing records.

Logically, one should expect that MARC would provide a format for descriptive records of primary sources in archival documents, private papers held in libraries, and manuscripts in library collections. Indeed guidelines for such a format have been written by Steven Hensen (1983) and discussed by Nancy Sahli, (1985). During the five years since its publication, the MARC-AMC format has come to be used by many libraries and archives for modern records, but seldom for cataloguing earlier documents (with the notable exception of the Research Libraries Group at The Rutgers University). The AMC Format may have been applied thus far by only two small manuscript collections in the U.S.A. with few manuscripts prior to 1500. Hope Mayo asks whether access to primary sources can be provided by libraries which depend exclusively upon MARC and the AMC format for cataloguing primary sources in manuscript, without thereby introducing new and excessive difficulties for researchers whose tasks are already very complex.

In this regard Lawrence McCrank is a bit more hopeful. Although all MARC records are organised in a monograph cataloguing format, McCrank points out that the MARC-AMC is a serial-based format which is more accommodating of archival compilations. With a MARC-record as a "boiler plate," the serial format of AMC allows for linkage of multiple descriptive records such as hypertext for the various parts of an early manuscript or printed book. Each linked record could have its own author, title, place and date of origin, and other attributions or critical appraisal. This would be more fitting for creating a catalogue record for the diversity of contents of most medieval and renaissance manuscript codices. The papers of Mayo and McCrank will be usefully read together in assessing the ways in which librarians may provide assistance for research into original sources with or without MARC. Further useful discussions were edited by Hope Mayo, "MARC Cataloging for Medieval Manuscripts," a special issue of *Rare Books & Manuscripts* 6/1 (1991), with articles by Mayo, Thomas Amos, Sara Lane, and Alexandra Mason.

Not all of the efforts to use computers for cataloguing manuscripts, rather than modern books, are accounted for in this collection of essays. A well conceived system in The Netherlands was created during the 1980s and denoted PCC, that is, "Producing Codicological Catalogues with the Aid of Computers," but it foundered for lack of funding (Gruijs, 1986). And the equally well conceived project ZIH, that is, the Zentralinventar mittelalterlicher Handschriften bis 1500, nearly went the same way due to lack of technical support as well as funding. Dr. Renate Schipke reports here that ZIH is recovering now and will survive for the benefit of all who wish to locate primary sources in manuscript collections found in the eastern provinces of Germany. Hopefully, its intentions to include incipits of texts found in all the manuscript collections of German lands will be realised. Another important catalogue of this sort is the Repertoire des incipits des manuscrits, organised by Jacqueline Hamesse (Louvain-la-Neuve) and Paul Bratley (Montréal); it is based at l'Institut d'études médiévales, Université catholique de Louvain, Belgium (Bratley, Hamesse 1990). Quite practical for libraries in the U.S.A. is the Research Libraries Information Network (RLIN) which is used by Research Libraries Group at Stanford, California. It intends to include both the ISTC and the ESTC, discussed here by Mayo.

Also serving the scholar who will draw upon original sources as they become available at his own computer-assisted workstation is a remarkable set of computer programmes with the Greek name, KLEIW, formerly CLIO. Under direction of Manfred Thaller and sponsored by the Max-Planck-Institut für Geschichte in Göttingen, Germany, KLEIW is available in a new MS-DOS version 3.1.1, and it serves several databases and provides excellent assistance to scholars in several countries (*Data Base*, 1988; Becker, 1989). Thus far, it does not include machine-readable cataloguing of manuscripts.

The first goal of any library must be to acquire and preserve an organised body of knowledge within its scope. University libraries and great national libraries give considerable emphasis to the mature levels of scholarship and to the body of knowledge needed by the most advanced students, university lecturers, young researchers early in their careers, and professors who are masters of their crafts. It provides a foundation for the structures of knowledge and understanding which they are building. They enable these scholars to acquire and preserve their own organised bodies of knowledge for research. In consequence the chambers of professors become rich in accumulated works and records which they have read and will read again, which they are analysing and interpreting. These are literary and historical workstations with specialised libraries from which will arise fresh discoveries and new publications.

Librarians however are usually better organised than the scholars they serve. Structured information is the strength of a great library which intends to provide support for scholarship in many or all fields of study. A good library will hold numerous old books and papers in the hundreds of thousands if not millions, but also it is always buying new books, receiving periodicals with very rich contents, and acquiring personal papers and manuscripts in such numbers that the user must wonder how anyone could possibly know what is there, how to find it, and how to preserve it for others. But the libraries are often so well organised that their structures do preserve their treasures and provide access to most of them quite efficiently by means of catalogues and reference tools.

Access to knowledge by means of the structured information provided by libraries is surely easier if it is found in quarto-format printed books than in other sorts of packages. It is less easy if those books have special characteristics and quite a bit more difficult if they were printed before A.D.1500. Great problems of access arise in a library when the information sought is to be found in unbound papers, printed or not, and it is the most difficult for information in manuscript, whether bound or not. There is diminishing access to books and manuscripts which are not printed and bound in quarto-format, and that impedes the work of scholars who are usually the most productive in any literary or historical fields of study.

All properly accredited scholars in literature and history are trained to take their research beyond the modern printed books which fill library shelves to overflowing, beyond even the latest published research in periodicals, until they reach the primary sources to be found in the surviving original manuscripts. Professors and leading scholars spend most of their research time and energies ferreting out new knowledge which others have not yet found, and they travel to any place where they can pour over the pages and turn through the folios of those original sources in manuscript which have been saved from destruction but which are also the very sources of knowledge which structured information systems of modern libraries make least accessible. As the papers of this ICHS Symposium suggest, such adverse organisation is not necessary. Better services for research scholars could be made available with computer-assisted cataloguing of primary sources in manuscript.

Many libraries have found that the application of computer technology to their catalogues has made modern printed books more readily available for users. They have developed machine-readable catalogues which can be searched on-line, for example "FELIX" in the University of Toronto libraries. There are also machine-readable indices and abstracts of periodical literature available by subscription in Biology, Chemistry, Law, and a wide variety of other disciplines. Some of these bibliographical tools are now available for literary and historical studies. Efforts are well advanced to prepare a systematic catalogue for the Incunable Short Title Catalogue (ISTC) in the British Library, London; and there is another for Eighteenth-century Short Title Catalogue of books in English (ESTC). But thus far, few libraries with collections of primary sources in manuscript have provided machine-readable catalogues, indices, or other reference tools for the aid of the users. For those librarians, archivists, and research scholars who believe that access to primary sources is the greatest value for sound research, this should be surprising.

The creators of machine-readable manuscript catalogues have been flexible in order to make the most effective use of the computer. By means of their new systems, they believe that the catalogue data may be searched and retrieved more efficiently. The research scholar would then need to spend less time for locating the form and content of many manuscripts and be able to work more on those contents themselves, the primary sources. But have the systems-creators lost sight of that remarkable conundrum of modern technology? As Susan Hockey pointed out, the computer may be more successful at finding information in a database than the human hand and eye could ever be, yet its very precision may actually defeat the search (Hockey, 1980). Information retrieval with the aid of a computer requires that there be exact correlation between the data defined for a search and the data which had been entered. Aye, ther's the rub! Hand, eye, and memory are able to recognise and accept variants or reject false similarities in the database; and it would be a forelorn hope that all possible variables of medieval, renaissance, and early modern onomastics could ever be exactly defined for the machine to recognise. Nevertheless, the technology of computers now allows one to search a database for natural language texts by truncation of prefixes or suffixes, by suspension of vowels within a word, or even by creation of pseudo-incipits; a pseudo-incipit is explained by Renate Schipke to be a series of initial letters from the first words of a text, rather than the words themselves, and this may be more efficient for locating that text in all manuscripts catalogued for the database than use of the proper incipit itself (p. 10). Human and machine may function together also when a database is searched interactively from a terminal. "Interactive'' has become a codeword for those who like the peculiar jargon of computer talk. But here it simply means that a machine-readable manuscript catalogue will be most effective when the research scholar is able to pose a question for search of the database, read the information retrieved, then rephrase the question or ask a new question in further searches until satisfied or sated.

Thus there are many fruitful ways to catalogue manuscript materials in machine-readable form for service to other research scholars. Reviewing these developments, Warren Van Egmond has compared computers in the twentieth century with printing presses in the fifteenth century. In each period, he believes, scholars recognized the new technology only as providing a faster means of doing what they were already doing and did not understand or use it very well. Cataloguing is in this early stage. The existing MARC format for library information serves for mass distribution of standardized data in old ways, says Van Egmond, but is inadequate to the task of disseminating cataloguing information on manuscript books. He encourages the development of special formats for these materials by a fuller realisation of the fuller potential of computers. An immediate result of the Symposium on ''Computer Programmes for Medieval and Renaissance Manuscript Sources'' has been the Manuscript Census Record (MCR) approach described by Amos in the last article of this collection. MCR will certainly appeal to librarians because it differentiates between ''First Level'' and ''Second Level'' descriptions of manuscripts. First level descriptions would fit nicely to the usual card catalogue type of data, and they could be communicated easily among the existing machine-readable manuscript catalogues, as well as between these systems and the usual library catalogues which draw upon MARC. This MCR would be a boon to scholars, as they search in their own library facilities for new and old materials on their research subjects throughout the world.

Opportunity for these papers to be presented for professional discussion was provided by Symposium S 3, ''Computer Programmes for Medieval and Renaissance Manuscript Sources,'' for the XVIIIth International Congress of History of Science, 1-9 August. My thanks are given to Professor Christoph J. Scriba (Hamburg), chairman of the Organising Committee, and to Professor Fritz Krafft (Marburg), chairman of the Programme Committee. The Symposium was sponsored by the International Union for History and Philosophy of Science, Commission on Bibliography, chairman Professor Renato Mazzolini (Trento). Final commentators were Professor Mazzolini and Professor Menso Folkerts (Munich). It met in three sessions: first in Hamburg on 5 August, and twice in Munich at the Deutsches Museum on 7 August where our generous host was Professor Folkerts, Institut für Geschichte der Naturwissenschaften der Universität München. The third session provided demonstrations of the Munich ICC MSM and of the MEDIUM on-line from Paris with the technical assistance of Drs. Andreas Kühne and Agnès Guillaumont. Finally our appreciation is also offered to the editor of *Primary Sources & Original Works*, Dean Lawrence J. McCrank, whose description of the Mt. Angel Abbey manuscripts with a customized computer programme (replacing FAMULUS) included phased cataloguing techniques, a step towards use of hypertext and serial formats in the development of rare book and machine-readable manuscript catalogues (McCrank and Batty, 1978).

REFERENCES

Amos, T.L. (1988). *The Manuscripts of the Fundo Alcobaça of the Biblioteca Nacional, Lisbon*, volume I: Manuscripts 1-150, Descriptive Inventories. Collegeville, Minnesota: The Hill Monastic Manuscript Library, Saint John's University Press.

———— (1989). Ibid., volume II: Manuscripts 151-301, Descriptive Inventories.

Becker, P. (1989). *KLEIW. Ein Tutorial*. Göttingen: Max-Planck-Institut für Geschichte.

Bratley, P. and Hamesse, J. (1990). "The Computerisation of Manuscript Incipits." In Choueka, Y. (Ed.), *Computers in Literary and Linguistic Research*. Actes de la XVe Conference Internationale, Jerusalem, 5-9 Juin 1988. Paris, Genève: Champion-Slatkine.

Folkerts, M. and Kühne, A. (Eds.) (1990). *The Use of Computers in Cataloging Medieval and Renaissance Manuscripts*. Papers from the International Workshop in Munich, 10-12 August 1989. *Algorismus*, *4*, pp. 19-40. Mühchen: Institut für Geschichte der Naturwissenschaften.

Gruijs, A. (1986). "L'informatique au service de la codicolographie: le SDDR dans le projet PCC à l'Université de Nimègue aux Pays-Bas." Ed. Härtel, H. et alii. *Wolfenbütteler Forschungen*, *30*, pp. 95-127. Wiesbaden: O.Harrassowitz.

Hensen, S. L. (1983). *Archives, Personal Papers, and Manuscripts: A Catalog-*

ing Manual for Archival Repositories, Historical Societies, and Manuscript Libraries. 1st edition (1983), 2nd edition (1989). Chicago: Society of American Archivists.

Hockey, Susan (1980). *A Guide to Computer Applications in the Humanities.* Baltimore, London: The Johns Hopkins University Press.

Kropac, I.H. and Leiter-Köhrer, U. (1989). *KLEIW. Der Datenbankeditor.* Göttingen: Max-Planck-Institut für Geschichte.

McCrank, L.J. and Batty, C.D. (1978). "The Mt. Angel Abbey Manuscript and Rare Books Project: Cataloguing with FAMULUS." In *Computers and the Humanities, 12,* pp. 215-222.

Sahli, N. (1985). *MARC for archives and manuscripts: the AMC format.* Chicago: The Society of American Archivists. Revised 1986.

Thaller, M. (1989). *KLEIW. 3.1.1. Ein Datenbanksystem.* Göttingen: Max-Planck-Institut für Geschichte.

Thaller, M. (Ed.) (1988). *Data Base Oriented Source Editions.* Göttingen: Max-Planck-Institut für Geschichte.

Three Steps
from Typewriter to Catalogue:
The Benjamin Catalogue
for the History of Science

Nan L. Hahn

SUMMARY. This paper reviews the recent history of computer-assisted cataloguing of early manuscripts and summarizes the origin and current status of five such projects. It discusses in detail the Benjamin Catalogue for the History of Science and in less detail the International Computer Catalogue of Medieval Scientific Manuscripts.

The Benjamin Catalogue was begun by the late Francis S. Benjamin who compiled 17,600 descriptions of Latin manuscripts written A.D.200-1800. These descriptions are extremely rich in their variety of sources, breadth of subjects, and depth of information. Since Benjamin's death in 1973 the project has been continued by his former students, Nan L. Hahn and Wesley M. Stevens.

Three years of cataloguing and preservation of the collection were followed by the gradual development of a scheme for encoding the descriptions into machine-readable form. The result is a code of 110 data fields that has proved to be efficient for the researcher to use as well as for the computer to manage. The project uses the Biblio-

---

Nan L. Hahn is Co-director of the Benjamin Catalogue for the History of Science. She received her Doctorate of Philosophy in medieval history from Emory University in 1972. A student of the late Francis S. Benjamin, she worked with him on his proposed catalogue of medieval scientific manuscripts and succeeded him as head of the project upon his death. She taught history at the University of Nebraska at Omaha, was at the Rutgers University as director of the Benjamin Catalogue project, and is now an independent scholar in Dunellen, New Jersey. She has received support for her research from the American Philosophical Society, the National Endowment for the Humanities, the Alfred P. Sloan Foundation, and others. Her publications include *Medieval mensuration: Quadrans vetus and Geometrie due sunt partes principales* (1982) and articles on medieval astronomical and mathematical texts and computer applications for manuscript cataloguing.

graphic and Grouping System (BAG/2) by John B. Smith as its data management system.

The principals joined forces with the Munich-based ICC MSM in 1982, and the two groups have made their encoding systems compatible. They have shared descriptions of all encoded materials, and their cooperative effort has expanded to include three other manuscript projects. Since 1985 they have held three international workshops to advance cooperation among these groups.

The cataloguing of early manuscripts was historically a long, tedious task requiring thousands of slips of paper, a faithful if battered typewriter, reams of typing paper, boxes of erasers, bottles of correction fluid and much patience. Initially the advent of the computer brought few changes, early applications being mainly in scientific research. But around 1965 a small wave of humanistic applications for this new tool began to grow and eventually swept over the scholarly world. Soon, manuscript cataloguing became a long and still tedious task which now required thousands of megabytes of storage, a faithful if battered personal computer, reams of printer paper, printer ribbons and much patience . . . Nevertheless, many scholars found the new task to be an improvement over the old one, whether tedious or not; it provided the possibility of doing perhaps in just one lifetime what had previously required several generations of a long-lived organization such as a research institution or a religious order. By 1970 there were several humanities manuscript projects under way on both sides of the Atlantic. Some examples follow.

A Roman Law project, Verzeichnis der Handschriften zum Römischen Recht bis 1600 by Gero Dolezalek and Johannes A.C.J. Van de Wouw at the Max-Planck-Institut in Frankfurt, was completed in 1972 and published in 1973. Its purpose was a "world union summary catalogue of manuscripts concerning Roman law, with indices of authors, titles, incipit and explicit words, centuries, origins, gatherings, scribes and possessors" (Dolezalek and Van de Wouw, 1972, p. 58).

An index project related to the Frankfurt work was begun at the University of California at Berkeley in 1976. Under the direction of Stephan Kuttner, the purpose of this project was to create a series of indices of various kinds for the Roman and canon law manuscripts of the Vatican libraries. This project continues, and most of the research has been completed; volume 3 will soon be in print, and at least two other volumes are in progress (Kuttner, 1976, p. 28).[1]

In 1971 Professor Walter M. Hayes of the Pontifical Institute of Mediaeval Studies, Toronto, announced an author-title survey of previously catalogued Greek manuscripts which is being continued there by Robert Sinkewicz (Hayes, 1971, p. 16; Sinkewicz, 1987). This work is projected to encompass fifty printed volumes. Similar work has been initiated by another group in the Netherlands (Hayes, 1976, p. 34-44; Dolezalek, 1979, p. 20).

In 1971 Canon A.L. Gabriel of the Mediaeval Institute, University of Notre Dame, announced completion of a catalogue of fifty Medieval and Renaissance manuscripts of the Biblioteca Ambrosiana in Milan. The purpose of the project was ''to provide a 'model' catalogue giving information on incipits, author, titles, dates, copyists, sizes of the manuscripts'' (p. 11). The result is very useful, but its limitations have prevented its becoming the model for computerized catalogues that the author intended.

In Paris, various computer-assisted projects based on medieval manuscripts began around 1970 at the Institut de Recherche et d'Histoire des Textes (IRHT) of the Centre National de la Recherche Scientifique (CNRS). Mme. Marie-José Beaud and Mme. Lucie Fossier began a major cataloguing project in 1973: the registration and description of 41,000 medieval manuscripts on microfilm in the collection of the IRHT. This project continues today under Agnès Guillaumont and Jean-Luc Minel as a relational database called MEDIUM. The format allows the user to search all the data repeatedly by menu, but the contents of each manuscript have been severely constricted. The wide range of information included in the original description may be available in conventional form through one of the IRHT sections, but machine-readable data are found only in limited fields for author, title, and date of each treatise in the manuscripts and a few other details (Guillaumont, Minel, 1991, 49-71). Elimination of incipits is particularly regrettable.

Of these and other computer-assisted manuscript-cataloguing endeavors that appeared in the literature between 1971 and 1980, many have gone by the wayside; some, like the Paris and Berkeley projects, continue today at varied rates of progress.

One of the continuing projects is the Benjamin Catalogue for the History of Science. Its origin and development reflect the history of many humanities projects undergoing computerization, and thus it may provide some guideposts for scholars beginning their work in the 1990s. The project has progressed in a slow and unsteady manner, occasionally halted but never abandoned. It began as a traditional typewritten collection of slips of paper in the late 1940s, and the use of a computer was under consideration by 1965. After several trials and errors during 1974-1977, successful application of computer to this mass of cataloguing information began in 1978. The project continues and has encoded in its database the descriptions of some 6,000 scientific manuscripts from the period A.D. 200-1800.

Formerly called "The Benjamin Data Bank of Medieval Scientific Manuscripts in Latin," our project was recently renamed to reflect more accurately its format and holdings as a summary catalogue. The original collection of information was the work of one scholar over a thirty year span: the late Francis S. Benjamin, medievalist and historian of science at Emory University; but five other scholars have contributed their descriptive information about those and additional manuscripts in the meantime. Source materials include descriptions of about 14,000 manuscripts written between 200 and 1400 A.D. and several thousands from 1400 to 1800. The manuscripts described are in western vernacular languages as well as in Latin. While their texts are primarily Latin, there are many items in Greek, Hebrew, Arabic, and the medieval and early modern vernacular languages as well.

Professor Benjamin began collecting manuscript descriptions for his own research while studying with Lynn Thorndike at Columbia University, and he continued this practice throughout his teaching career.[2] Using these materials, he produced a number of scholarly works, the most notable being his edition of Campanus of Novara's *Theorica planetarum*, a major thirteenth-century text on Ptolemaic astronomy (Benjamin and Toomer, 1971).

To acquire much of the information for his work, Benjamin purchased and borrowed hundreds of catalogues which he perused for any items on the history of science. He travelled to many American and European libraries to review manuscripts and catalogues that could not circulate through the mails. His early notes were written in his minute and difficult hand with either pencil or ink, but most of them were eventually transcribed in typed form. By the time of his death in 1973, his collection of typed slips had grown to some 20,000 sheets containing more than 17,600 manuscript descriptions.

In addition to his own research, Benjamin maintained an international correspondence with other scholars in his field. Among them were Lynn Thorndike, Pearl Kibre, Marshall Clagett, Gerald Toomer and many European scholars and librarians; their contributions added much to his collection of descriptive information about the manuscripts.

Expanding the collection beyond his own research area and making the materials available to others were two goals that Benjamin adopted early on. To a major U.S. foundation in 1949, he stated: "I propose to do for the Roman libraries what Ernst Zinner [in his catalogue of astronomical manuscripts] . . . did for the German libraries, but more completely in view of the narrower scope."[3] He did not complete this task, but his Roman collection, including Vatican manuscripts, ultimately totalled some 1,100 descriptions.

Benjamin's expansion of the breadth of his data base can clearly be seen in his descriptions. The collection is naturally strong in his own research area, medieval astronomy, but it is not limited to that. More importantly, it includes all topics within the broadest possible definition of science and technology as defined in the period under study. There is no omission of astrology, necromancy, divination and the like because of modern views of "science"; judgements of what belongs in the collection are based on a view moving forward from the Classical period rather than backward from modern times.

Benjamin gathered far more types of information about the texts than were usually found in most well-known catalogues; this may be seen in the list of fields or categories into which we place this information. Frequently there appears at the top of a manuscript description a brief notation of one or two scientific items in the manuscript, taken from the first source of information available to him. A second, more elaborate description from a later period details everything in the manuscript down to and including small marginalia, flyleaf notes, and everything else between the covers. This description would be taken from the manuscript itself, from a microfilm copy, or from the detailed description in a modern catalogue by then available to him. And he enriched his descriptions with citations of hundreds of other scholarly sources. We have learned from him that a truly useful bibliographic tool must include all possible information, both original and referential; we cannot restrict future scholars as to what fields should or should not be available in a database for them to search.

Benjamin's growing interest in the contents of entire manuscripts led to the purchase of numerous microfilms from large and small libraries and from collections throughout western and eastern Europe and North America. The study of many of them enabled him to expand earlier, sketchy descriptions drawn from catalogues and other sources. These films, now numbering some 170,000 exposures, are an invaluable source to us for verifying old descriptions and making new ones. Again, his wisdom in collecting copies of the original materials for repeated study and verification has contributed greatly to the quality of our final product.

Although Benjamin's goal of developing a scholarly research tool was defined by 1950, the current methodology was not; indeed, it did not exist. Benjamin considered computerization from about 1965 onward, but he delegated that task to me as his junior associate. But a long illness ending in his death in 1973 left the entire project unrealised. I quickly brought another former Benjamin student, Professor Wesley M. Stevens of the University of Winnipeg, into the plans as co-director.

Identification, sorting and conserving the Benjamin materials began in 1974 at the University of Nebraska at Omaha.[4] Many were fading and crumbling and most needed corrections of errors, and missing letters or overstrikes, requiring two years of concentrated labor.[5] As a safeguard against any disaster, I produced a second copy of the papers and placed it with my partner at his Canadian university.

The decision to enlarge our data base to include the contributions of other scholars was a natural outgrowth of our having been students of Benjamin; we first added our own descriptions, begun under his tutelage. As we shared our plans with other scholars, several of them responded by offering their own scholarly notes. Among them were Professors Marshall Clagett, Charles Jones, James A. Weisheipl, Michael Mahoney, and Thomas Izbicki. All of these greatly broadened and enriched our corpus of materials.

We began experimenting with locally available equipment and methods of computerization in 1975, but these proved to be very inadequate. The major sources of information today, the professional organizations, newsletters, journals and local computer clubs, were not then available. Realizing that we needed hardware dedicated to our project, more sophisticated software, labor, work space and released time for me to develop the project, we began seeking outside support. In 1977 the National Endowment for the Humanities (NEH) agreed to fund us for a time if we would find and use existing software rather than pay for the development of our own.[6] This seemingly impossible task was facilitated by our relocation to Rutgers University in the midst of a geographic area with many excellent professional specialists. Professor John B. Smith, then of The Pennsylvania State University, generously gave us a group of his programs called the BAG/2 System (Smith, 1982). Installed in 1979, this system was so advanced that the revised version of 1982 continues to meet our needs very well. Still before the era of the personal computer, we purchased and used for four years a mini-computer for data entry and editing and to serve as a remote station for the university host computer.

The most demanding step was to determine the specific fields of data and then to develop the rules for encoding the diverse information supplied by the manuscript descriptions in our holdings. This task required a year. We first reviewed a number of manuscript catalogues, searching for a suitable format. Solutions for specific problems were available, such as methods of entering in machine-readable form the many different expressions of dates used by cataloguers who were more or less summary, trained or untrained in paleography and codicology, and who made their decisions about detail during various periods of the development of those crafts. But we found no general plan that could satisfy the essential requirements for the database of a machine-readable manuscript catalogue. These were:

1. that it provide a field or home for every piece of information given to us;
2. that it encompass the many varied forms of the manuscript descriptions received from existing catalogues and inventories and yet be consistent enough to be machine-readable; and
3. that the total list of fields be short enough to be learned and used efficiently by an encoder.

Our solution was to develop a format with two major areas: a general manuscript section, or "header"; and an item section for each entity within the manuscript, whether it be a text, table, chart, drawing or some other type of information. The header would include all data that applied to the entire manuscript. Each item section would include all data pertaining to that item. This field list has recently been revised and is given below in the APPENDIX. To ensure uniformity in the work of encoders, a manual on the project, its software, the data fields and their encoding protocols was produced.[7]

The period at Rutgers was very productive during 1978-1981, and its computer facilities and personnel gave excellent assistance to this natural language work. Unfortunately, administrative and funding problems during 1981-1982 made it impossible for the project to sustain itself there. The University of Winnipeg became the sponsor in May 1983, and funds became available to establish offices and equipment both in Dunellen, New Jersey and in Winnipeg, Manitoba. At this time we became associated with the International Computer Catalogue of Medieval Scientific Manuscripts (ICC MSM) at the Deutsches Museum in Munich, directed by Professor Menso Folkerts.

Since that time the Benjamin Catalogue and the ICC MSM have cooperated by sharing manuscript descriptions in the form of processed data, avoiding duplication of labor and waste, and close consultation. To enable smooth and efficient transfer of data, we arranged for all three offices (Dunellen, Winnipeg, and Munich) to have the same software (Nota Bene) and similar hardware (IBM PC XT or AT and compatible PCs). All files are stored in pure ASCII values. Overall concepts for mutually compatible projects were agreed upon. Each of the three offices would send and receive copies of all of previously encoded manuscript descriptions from the other two and new descriptions as they were completed; manuscript lists were exchanged to avoid duplication of work. Each office also agreed to keep current backup copies of all data at an offsite location. We thus are assured that all data are in a universal format and that they can be moved both laterally among the projects and vertically to newer and more sophisticated systems as these become available to us. This makes the completion of our task a possibility within the foreseeable future.

By 1985 both projects had encoded large amounts of data but with separate encoding systems. They seemed to be quite similar, yet they gave somewhat different emphases to the texts and to the make up of manuscript codices. Therefore the agreed exchange of manuscript descriptions was seriously hindered. One solution appeared to be a merger of the two systems of fields and encoding protocols into one which would be all inclusive. We soon found however that this would be very cumbersome.

Professor Stevens invited representatives from four manuscript projects to meet 19-23 October 1986 in Winnipeg for a Workshop sponsored by the University of Winnipeg and the Social Sciences Research Council of Canada. Sharing their expertise were Professor Menso Folkerts (University of Munich), Dr. Thomas L. Amos of the Hill Monastic Manuscript Library (Saint John's University, Minnesota), Professor Serge Lusignan of the Institut d'études médiévales (Université Montréal), Professor John B. Smith (now University of North Carolina and author of the BAG/2 System), Professor Warren Van Egmond (Arizona State University at Tempe and author of the ICC MSM encoding system), with Stevens and myself. We seven worked four days to review hardware; the BAG/2 and other software programmes; normalisations of spellings; multiple authors, titles, incipits and explicits; dating systems; commentaries and translations; and other matters. Far too many bits of useful information had been placed by encoders in a field called "Other information." Furthermore the two projects had somewhat different foci, based on the thrusts of their collections: the ICC MSM materials included much greater detail on the codicological aspects of the manuscripts, and the Benjamin collection provided far more detail on their contents. Thus the Winnipeg Workshop agreed that a consolidated code large enough to encompass all previously processed materials would be impractical. Rather, it was thought that parallel plans for retrospective conversion would allow each project to absorb the other's data with less difficulty. In addition the Benjamin Catalogue agreed to reorder its fields and restate its encoding protocols, and this has been carried out.

In order to formalize our association with these advisers and other interested scholars, we established a Board of Contributors: a group to consult for advice and manuscript information. A common practice with projects like ours, this has become a source of great strength for the directors. Professor Folkerts was asked to be Associate Director of the project. We made plans for the Benjamin Catalogue to publish occasional papers called *Questio de rerum natura*, edited by Wesley M. Stevens. This publishes original monographs about primary sources in manuscript for History of Science in ancient, classical, medieval, and early modern Europe. Three issues of *Questio* are now available.[8]

Since the 1986 meeting, the Benjamin Catalogue and the ICC MSM have continued to cooperate. Professor Stevens organised the Symposium for the International Congress of History of Science, the papers from which form the present volume. Professor Folkerts organised a Workshop for about thirty participants in Munich, 10-12 August 1989, sponsored by the Deutsches Museum.[9] Dr. Hahn organised a Symposium for the International Congress of the Association for Computers in History and the Association for Literary and Linguistic Computing or ACH/ACCL which met jointly in Siegen, Germany, 5-9 June 1990. The purpose of each symposium and workshop was to broaden our base of cooperating projects, and much progress was made. In each of them additional manuscript projects were represented, and the scope of machine-readable manuscript catalogues has become better understood.

At this time the Benjamin Catalogue has encoded some 6,000 manuscript descriptions and the Munich project has completed some 9,175. The Munich office has been executing searches for about a year, and the Benjamin Catalogue expects that funding for this service to scholars may be available in the summer of 1991; requests may be sent to Professor Stevens.[10]

NOTES

1. Telephone interview (Dec. 22, 1989) with Stephanie Tibbets of the Institute of Canon Law at Berkeley.

2. Benjamin's interest in manuscript identification is typical of members of the circle around Professor Thorndike in the pre- and postwar era. Among Thorndike students during this period were Pearl Kibre, Marshall Clagett, Gerald

Toomer, and Richard LeMay, all scholars vitally interested in this area of research.

3. Correspondence with the Fulbright Educational Program for the academic year 1951-52; undated files in the Benjamin Catalogue for Medieval Science.

4. Assistance was received by a grant from the Faculty Senate of the University of Nebraska at Omaha.

5. Photocopying of the Benjamin Papers was assisted by a grant from the American Philosophical Society.

6. National Endowment for the Humanities, grant number RT-33000-78-1173, granted August 31, 1978.

7. Some two hundred copies have been distributed, and a new edition is in progress.

8. Issues of *Questio de rerum natura* are:

  I. Nan L. Hahn *et alii.* The Benjamin Data Bank and BAG/2 (1983, 1985), iii + 102 pages.
  II. Menso Folkerts, Euclid in medieval Europe (1989), 63 pages.
  III. Serge Lusignan. The Reception of Vincent Beauvais in Langue d'oil (1989), 20 pages.

They are available from Overdale Books, 269 Overdale Road, Winnipeg, Manitoba, R3J 2G2, CANADA.

9. The papers have been published as *The Use of Computers in Cataloging Medieval and Renaissance Manuscripts,* edited by M. Folkerts and A. Kühne (1990).

10. Professor W. M. Stevens, University of Winnipeg, Winnipeg, Manitoba R3B 2E9, CANADA; electronic mailing address: UOWWMS@UOFMCC.Netnorth.Bitnet.

REFERENCES

Benjamin, F. S., Jr. and Toomer, G. J. (1971). *Campanus of Novara and Medieval Planetary Theory: Theorica Planetarum.* Madison, Wisconsin.

Dolezalek, G. (1979). Recension des travaux concernant des catégories particulières de manuscrits—et, principalement, ceux qui utulisent l'informatique. *CAMDAP,* 9, 1, p.20.

Dolezalek, G. and Van de Wouw, J. (1972). In *CAMDAP,* 2, 2, p.58.

Folkerts, M. and Kühne, A. (Eds.) (1990). *The Use of Computers in Cataloging Medieval and Renaissance Manuscripts* (1990). Papers from the International Workshop in Munich, 10-12 August 1989. In *Algorismus,* 6, Studien zur Geschichte der Mathematik und der Naturwissenschaften, hsg. M. Folkerts. München: Institut für Geschichte der Naturwissenschaften.

Gabriel, A. L. (1971). Manuscripts of the Ambrosiana. *CAMDAP,* 1, 2, p.11.

Hahn, N. L., Smith, J. B., Stevens, W. M. and Sorenson, B. L. (1983). *The Benjamin Data Bank and BAG/2: A Case History and User Manual for Encod-*

ing, Storing, and Retrieving Information on Medieval Manuscripts. Winnipeg: Overdale Books.

Hayes, W. M. (1971). An author-title survey of catalogued Greek manuscripts. In *CAMDAP, 1*, 2, p.16.

———— (1976). Author-name work-title index of printed catalogues of Greek manuscripts. In *CAMDAP*, 6, 2, pp.43-44.

Kuttner, S. (1976). Index to the Vatican libraries' holdings in Roman and canon law manuscripts. In *CAMDAP*, 6, p.28.

Sinkewicz, R. E. (1987). *The Greek Index Project: A Report*. Toronto: The Pontifical Institute of Mediaeval Studies.

Smith, J. B. (1982). *BAG/2: A Bibliographic and Grouping System for Natural Language Data*, revised. Pennsylvania: Pennsylvania State University Computation Center.

Zinner, E. (1925). *Verzeichnis der Astronomischen Handschriften des Deutschen Kulturgebietes*. München: Verlag C.H. Beck.

APPENDIX

The core of the Benjamin Catalogue is the data field system with its encoding system for entering information into fields where it may be found and retrieved by the research scholar. The system is three-tiered. The first tier gives the immediate source of the descriptive data; thus %01 signifies that the data is entered from the Benjamin Papers; %02 signifies Clagett Papers; %03 C.W. Jones Papers; %04 W.M. Stevens Papers; and so forth. Following the repeated siglum % and a point, both of which are necessary, are data fields of second and third tiers. The chart lists second tier fields %.01 - %.50 which control information about the manuscript as a whole codex, called the "header" because its information will be provided along with other retrieved data about any item in the manuscript. Third tier fields %.51 - %.99 control information about each individual treatise or other single item, such as a commentary, gloss, chart, or drawing. Fields %.51 - %.99 will be repeated for each additional item in the codex.

Note further that in this system each field is capable of expansion to receive and produce data of any desired amount, the upper limit being imposed only by practical considerations of utility and search time.

BENJAMIN CATALOGUE
FOR THE HISTORY OF SCIENCE

FIELD LIST

July 1989

%01 Collection = e.g., Benjamin Papers
HEADER = Codicology
    %.01 City, province or state, and country
    %.02 Library or other owner
    %.03 Special collection and shelfmark
    %.04 Other identification marks
    %.05 Name or short title of manuscript
    %.06 Date of writing the codex
        %.06.01 Mode of dating.
        %.07 - %.08 Not in use
        %.09 Folios and format
        %.10 Physical make up, additional information
        %.10.01 Manuscript material, abbreviate:
                P = paper, papier, chartaceus,
                PE = parchment, pergamentum, membranaceus,
                V = vellum.
        %.10.02 Signatures or gatherings.
        %.10.03 Watermarks.
        %.10.04 Binding formula: cover, pastedowns, guard sheets, fly leaves.
        %.10.05 Binding material and markings.
        %.10.06 Remarks on any damaged leaves and the general condition of the manuscript.
        %.10.07 Composite manuscripts.
    %.11 Paleography
        %.11.01 Number of hands.
        %.11.02 Style of hand.
        %.11.03 Sigla and/or name of scribe, and location on folios.
        %.11.04 Number of columns; marking and width of columns.
        %.11.05 Marking, number, and overall height of lines.

%.11.06 Color of ink(s).

%.11.07 Use of rubrics, paragraph marks, initials, capitals, etc.

%.11.08 Illuminations, illustrations, drawings, diagrams.

%.11.09 Marginalia; other remarks on the paleography of the manuscript.

%.12 History of the manuscript

%.12.01 Owners' notes written in the manuscript.

%.12.02 Coats-of-arms.

%.12.03 Ex-libris plates, library stamps.

%.12.04 Origin.

%.12.05 Provenance.

%.12.06 Previous owners or users.

%.12.07 Date of most recent acquisition.

%.13 Bibliographic information about the codex

%.13.01 Catalogues describing this codex.

%.13.02 Descriptions of the codex in other published works.

%.13.03 Printed editions of the codex.

%.13.04 Facsimile editions of the codex.

%.13.05 Microfilm or other photocopies.

%.13.06 Work in progress on this codex.

%.13.07 Other notes of interest.

%.14 Language(s)

%.15 Genre(s)

%.16 Sub-genre

%.17 Type of manuscript

%.18 - %.19 Fields not currently in use

%.20 Other remarks about the description

%.21 - %.39 Fields not currently in use

%.40 - %.42 Categories of information about the source of the material in the collection of research papers being used (e.g., Benjamin's sources)

%.40 Contributor

%.41 Type of data in research paper

%.42 Source of data

%.43 - %.50 Fields not used at present

END OF HEADER

CONTENT OF INDIVIDUAL ITEMS
%.51 Folios for the item.
%.52 Author(s)
%.52.01 Author(s) – variant name or spelling.
%.52.02 Author of dedication.
%.52.03 Author of prologue.
%.52.04 Author of first portion of text.
%.52.05 Author of second portion of text.
%.52.06 Author of third portion of text.
%.52.07 Author of non-textual material. (e.g., tables, indexes).
%.52.08 Commentator.
%.52.09 Translator.
%.52.10 Editor.
%.53 Title(s)
%.53.02 Title of dedication
%.53.03 Title of prologue
%.53.04 Title of first portion of text
%.53.05 Title of second portion of text
%.53.06 Title of third portion of text
%.53.07 Title of non-textual material (e.g., tables, indexes)
%.53.08 Title of commentary.
%.54 Incipit
%.54.02 Initial line of dedication.
%.54.03 Initial line of prologue.
%.54.04 First incipit (first line) of text.
%.54.05 Second incipit of text.
%.54.06 Third incipit of text.
%.54.07 Initial line of non-textual material (e.g., tables, indexes, calendars).
%.54.08 Incipit of commentary.
%.55 Explicit
%.55.02 Explicit (last line) of dedication.
%.55.03 Explicit of prologue.
%.55.04 Explicit of first portion of text.
%.55.05 Explicit of second portion of text.
%.55.06 Explicit of third portion of text.
%.55.07 Explicit of non-textual material (e.g., tables, indexes).

%.55.08 Explicit of commentary.
%.55.09 Explicit of translator's remarks.
%.55.10 Explicit of editor's remarks.
%.55.11 Colophon.
%.56 Handling of an incomplete item
%.57 Description number on upper corner of paper
%.58 Not in use
%.59 Additional Material on Folio
    %.59.01 Minor texts within or following main text.
    %.59.02 Glossa, scholia, commentaries.
    %.59.03 Tables, lists, indices, appendices, etc.
    %.59.04 Illuminations (painted), illustrations (colored), line drawings (uncolored); diagrams, mathematical, astronomical or other.
    %.59.06 Musical notations.
    %.59.07 Doodles, scribbles, other markings.
    %.59.08 Catchword.
    %.59.09 Blank pages, or damaged or imperfect.
%.60 - %.63   Fields not used at present
%.64 - %.75 Variations in item data: Composite or single manuscripts which are composed of dissimilar items
%.64 Language(s) other than Latin. cf. %.14
%.65 Date of writing. cf. %.06
%.66 Origin. cf. %.12.04
%.67 Provenance. cf. %.08
%.68 Previous owners or users. cf. %.12.06
%.69 Folios, size, format. cf. %.09
%.70 Manuscript material. cf. %.10.01
%.71 Paleography. cf. %.11
    %.71.01 Number of hands. cf. %.11.01
    %.71.02 Style of hands. cf. %.11.02.
    %.71.03 Sigla and/or name of scribe, and location on folios. cf. %.11.03.
    %.71.04 Number, marking and width of columns. cf. %.11.04.
    %.71.05 Number, marking and overall height of line space. cf. %.11.05.
    %.71.06 Color of ink(s). cf. %.11.06.

%.71.07 Rubrics, paragraph marks, initials, capitals, etc. cf. %.11.07.

%.71.08 Not in use.

%.71.09 Other remarks on paleography of text. cf. %.11.09.

%.72 Type of data. cf. %.41

%.73 Source of data. cf. %.42

%.74 Photocopy location. cf. %.13.05

%.75 Work in progress. cf. %.13.06

%.76 - %.79 Fields not used at present

%.80 Bibliography of this text

%.81 Other manuscript copies of this text

%.82 Other remarks about this item

%.83 - %.99 Fields not used at present

%END OF RECORD

MEDIUM:
Database for Medieval Manuscripts

Agnès Guillaumont
Jean-Luc Minel

SUMMARY. Since its foundation in 1937, the Institut de Recherche et d'Histoire des Textes has been acquiring microfilms of manuscripts from libraries around the world. Today the film library of IRHT possesses more than 41,000 microfilms. The manuscripts are analyzed at the Institut and the resulting descriptions provide the principle elements for the MEDIUM relational database. By consulting the database, a researcher can trace the various copies of classical or medieval works, as well as the translations or commentaries they have engendered. The linguistic range includes Latin, Greek, old French and Provençal, Arabic, Hebrew, and to a lesser extent oriental Christian languages and the medieval Slavic and Celtic languages. Thematic inquiries are also possible since the works are identified by a two-tiered thematic indexation (generic and specific).

Agnès Guillaumont is Director of the Computer Department of the Institut de Recherche et d'Histoire des Textes (Centre national de la recherche scientifique). She is engaged in the conception and development of databases within the domain of manuscript analysis and historical data.

Jean-Luc Minel is Software Engineer in the Computer Department of the Institut de Recherche et d'Histoire des Textes, and Technical Consultant at the French National Administration College (ENA). For several years he has participated in the conception and development of databases and expert systems for use of administrative dossiers, management systems, and analysis of historical documents, as well as in projects which are aimed at the integration of expert systems with conventional information systems.

An early version of this paper was presented by A. Guillaumont for the International Congress of History of Science on 7 August 1989 in Munich and again for an International Workshop in Munich, 10-12 August, 1989, "Medium, base de données sur le manuscrit médiéval. Un exemple d'application en histoire des sciences," which appeared in *The Use of Computers in Cataloging* (1990), pp. 57-64. The authors wish to thank Professor Wesley M. Stevens (Winnipeg) for advice about further development and revisions of this paper and for his assistance with the English translation.

The MEDIUM database is accessible by means of any terminal or personal computer linked up to a telecommunications network.

MEDIUM is a general database for the medieval manuscript, conceived for the purpose of tracing the transmission of a text through its various copies, translations and commentaries. It is not specially oriented for studies in any one field and does not claim to be exhaustive in any of them. The database contains descriptions of manuscripts in all disciplines and in all occidental and oriental languages of the Mediterranean basin from the eighth to the fifteenth century. A research scholar may well be interested in MEDIUM's encyclopedic, linguistic and chronological extensions.

A creation of the Institut de Recherche et d'Histoire des Textes, MEDIUM reflects the work performed there. Founded in 1937, the IRHT studies the transmission of texts from antiquity until the invention of printing and the onset of the Renaissance. The object of these studies is the medieval manuscript both as a unique artifact and as bearer of the written word. The IRHT has created the following research resources:

- a worldwide census of manuscripts in public and private libraries and repositories
- a film library
- an archive containing an exhaustive description of each manuscript
- an archive of bibliographic documentation.

These undertakings are made available to scholars through a film library containing 50,000 microfilms; published inventories and catalogues; descriptions of manuscripts; more than 1,000,000 entries on card files; computer files and bibliographic databases; and the MEDIUM database.

The Institut employs 100 people in three locations, one in Orléans and two in Paris. It is divided into linguistic sections: Latin, Greek, Old French and Provençal, Arabic, Hebrew, with specialists in Slavic, Celtic, and oriental Christian languages; and thematic sections: Paleography, Codicology, Humanism, Diplomatic, Iconography, Musicology, and Heraldry. The same divisions for multidisciplinary research are found in the MEDIUM database.

For many years at IRHT, we have tried to work out the most appropriated methods for describing medieval manuscripts. A systematic and exhaustive method of description was conceived by Mme. Marie-José Beaud and Mme. Lucie Fossier and developed during several years of consultations with groups of experts under the auspices of the Institute. These collective studies have led to the composition in 1977 of a Guide which is still available in Dutch, English, French, Italian, and Russian: *Guide for writing a manuscript description*, edited by L. Fossier, M.-J. Beaud, *et alii*.

However in 1973 Mme. Fossier and Mme. Beaud also began to create machine readable files for more limited descriptions of manuscripts. This took the form of a sequential index or flat-file. This concept was given a new life in 1980 by the creation of a relational database, MEDIUM, in order to allow more rapid and interactive consultation of the data.

MEDIUM: CONTENTS

Definition of the Corpus

The manuscripts for which IRHT has a microfilm also are accompanied by descriptions which have been established from the microfilm and which have often been verified directly from the manuscript itself. The corpus could be extended to include descriptions of manuscripts not available on microfilm at IRHT, and certain authors are already thus represented. The film library has been built up from the specific requests for films made by scholars and therefore is much richer in some areas (Patristic Literature for example) than in others.

MEDIUM contains information from those descriptions from 41,000 microfilms of manuscripts at IRHT. The original manuscripts themselves are located in 1195 repositories at 614 cities scattered through some 50 countries. Of these, the contents of 25,000 texts from only 10,500 of the manuscripts have been described, thus far. The number of authors cited is 2738.

The database is translinguistic, encompassing all Mediterranean culture, East and West, from the eighth to the fifteenth century. Twenty-four languages are represented. We are conscious of the problems posed by such a diversity of material and the difficulties in finding a common terminology for the description of Latin, Greek, French, Arabic and Hebrew manuscripts. However ME-DIUM does not attempt to give a complete codicological description of each manuscript, but rather provides access to the contents from different points of view, eventually referring the interrogator back to the complete descriptions in files of the individual sections of IRHT. Access to texts is our prime objective, and this explains the importance attached to the normalization of the names of authors, titles, and written forms for transliteration of Arabic and Hebrew, as well as Latin forms of Greek.

Access to the Database

MEDIUM is consulted through conversational enquiry. The interrogation takes place using dialogue menus that propose the different points of access for the user. Several users can make interrogations and up-datings simultaneously; the programme untangles any conflicts of access.

MEDIUM is necessarily multi-site and multi-station because the IRHT is geographically spread out. But it is also accessible in France and abroad for simple query or for on-line enquiries by means of any terminal or personal computer linked up to TRANS-PAC, EURONET, or most other telecommunications networks. In addition to conversational access, we are also able to publish catalogues upon demand, and can extract subsets of the data onto floppy-discs for further research.

MEDIUM: CONSTRUCTION

The computer programme called MEDIUM was developed by Agnès Guillaumont and Jean-Luc Minel of the Computer Section of IRHT. It uses as its point of departure the database management system ADABAS which is distributed by the German company Software AG. It is installed on the IBM host computer at the Centre de Calcul du CNRS at Orsay (CIRCE).

Architecture of the Database

MEDIUM is a relational database in which a homogeneous grouping of information constitutes an entity or a single file. The individual
records in any one entity can be linked with those in another entity.
Such a model has the advantage of avoiding repetitions of the same
data: any given medieval text for example need be recorded only
once and is automatically cross-referenced to each manuscript in
which it appears. Relational programming also allows for user
friendly controls for the sake of coherency and validity. As data are
entered for example, the program checks in the recorded data
whether the author is already known, whether the shelfmark is
properly formulated, and so on. This results in entities whose records are mutually consistent. Furthermore this form of relational
database has the advantage that retrieval operations are not affected
by the quantity of data stored in MEDIUM.

The principle entities in the MEDIUM programme describe the
manuscript as a whole and identify the microfilm in the IRHT film
library. For each text there is information about the work as it appears in the manuscript. In the case of a translation or a commentary, there is citation of the original text on which it is based. And
there will be complementary or bibliographic information concerning each text. A detailed listing of the information contained in each
entity is given in appendix at the end of this article.

There are also three particularly important problems to be discussed.

Normalization and Consultation Aids

Major problems posed by the diversity of appellations, multiplic-
ity of spellings for the names of authors, and variants for titles are
resolved in the following way:

The first step is that of normalization—a disputed step but indispensable. For this we use standard reference works acknowledged
by experts for each period.

The second step is the creation of consultation aids. Normalization is of little help if the user of the database is unfamiliar with the
choices that have been made and the rules that have been established. For the names of authors therefore, the user may call for
display all or part of the master list. There are also automatic cross-

references; in principle, an author is designated by a single normalized form and cross-referenced to secondary forms (e.g., ALANUS AURIGA is cross-referenced automatically to ALAIN CHARTIER). In the case of completely different linguistic fields however, such as Arabic and Latin, two normalized forms are listed with mutual cross-references (e.g., AVICENNA and IBN SîNâ).

In search for titles, the enquiry is made by means of a character string which helps eliminate the unstable elements in a title. In an effort to offer a supplementary access to anonymous works which are particularly difficult to recover, we are currently working on a form of access that will sort out the proper names of persons and places embedded in titles.

MEDIUM does not at present contain *incipits*. The entity has been created for this purpose but is still being tested, and there are major hurdles to be overcome. For a manuscript collection as vast and varied as that of IRHT, it is necessary to define the rules by which the entity may be applied: where does an incipit begin or end? One problem is posed by formulaic incipits, another by texts having one or more prologue or preface. How much should one normalize incipits?

Nomenclature

Each work is characterized in MEDIUM by a two-tiered thematic indexation: generic and specific. As with any thesaurus, the establishment of this nomenclature has been a delicate task. It still has imperfections and is subject to criticism. Often the analysts at IRHT are called upon to examine texts that have never before been described or catalogued. Characterization of the content of a text presupposes the choice of a level of analysis. This level is determined by the analysts' knowledge of the users' needs and desires. Regardless of shortcomings of this nomenclature, its value is comparable to that of a subject index in bibliographical research; a thematic structure is one of the few ways of bringing together scattered, little known texts.

Translations and Commentaries

A large number of medieval works are translations or commentaries. In the case of a multi-lingual database such as MEDIUM, it is particularly interesting to be able to trace the successive transformations of a text. For this reason, the entity *Oeuvre* or "the written work" is associated with the entity *Oeuvre Originelle* or "the original written work." In the present model for MEDIUM, the text as it appears in the manuscript is given prime position (i.e., displayed first). In the case of a translation or commentary, the author is thus considered to be the translator or commentator. This approach is both proper and practical because this person is often the only one explicitly named, and frequently the work he has performed on the original text has transformed it into yet another distinct work. (The perspective was reversed in the previous model for MEDIUM; the problem is one of the representation of knowledge).

MEDIUM: INTERROGATION

The user enters MEDIUM by a series of menus that offer a variety of choices and possibilities which will give access both to the manuscripts and to the texts. The different approaches correspond to several research criteria:

- place of conservation
- microfilm number
- date
- author's name
- title
- language
- nomenclature
- iconographique key words
- specialized criteria for diplomatic texts.

If the number of texts selected by the first criterion is too large, the question may be refined by using a second criterion. This limitation to two successive research criteria is voluntary, as it saves the researcher from having to use a Boolean type of query language, but the system of enquiry can be adjusted if necessary.

The traditional bibliographical tools are all specialized according to linguistic or other scholarly fields. A general, multi-lingual database such as MEDIUM offers a relational mode of enquiry. It breaks down barriers of language and discipline by providing for example an unrestricted grouping of all the works of one author, including scientific treatises as well as philosophical and mystical works for example of the venerable Beda or Avicenna or Albertus Magnus and many others. Similarly all sorts of old French texts containing medical recipes may be brought together.

The enquiry has greatest potential in the field of textual transmission when it allows a wealth of copies, translations and commentaries on a text to surface. The search may be assisted by combining the equivalences of an author's name in Latin, Arabic and Hebrew (e.g., Galenus — JâLîNûS, IBN MâSAWAYHI — JOHANNES MESUE), even if the problems of attribution have not always been resolved, especially in the case of extracts or fragments.

Rather than trusting in a theoretical description, you are invited to explore the MEDIUM database yourself (see Table 1).

TABLE 1

ARCHITECTURE OF THE DATABASE
STRUCTURE OF ENTITIES

MANUSCRIPT
MICROFILM

COUNTRY	FOLIOS FILMED
PLACE OF CONSERVATION	ENVELOPE NUMBER
LIBRARY	AMOUNT FILMED
SHELFMARK	NUMBER OF FRAMES
DATE OF MANUSCRIPT	PHOTO DATE
SECTION OF IRHT	PHOTO TYPE
DESCRIPTION	ARCHIVAL COPY
WRITING MATERIALS	OLIM
DIMENSIONS	OLD MICROFILM
OWNER'S SHELFMARK	OTHER FILM LIBRARY
BINDING	MICROFILMING
EX-LIBRIS	ORIGIN OF FILM
DECORATION	GIFT

COPY IN LIBRARY
ENLARGEMENT
PHOTOGRAPHS

WORK
AUTHOR

AUTHOR   NAME
TITLE   AUTHOR CROSS-REFERENCES
TITLE CROSS-REFERENCE
TYPOLOGY (Original text,   DATE
  Translation, Commentary)   CHRONOLOGY
LANGUAGE   QUALITY
FRAGMENT   ORDER
TO BE FURTHER ANALYZED
KEY WORD(S): GENERIC
KEY WORD(S): SPECIFIC

ORIGINAL WORK
DIPLOMATIC

ORIGINAL AUTHOR   RELIGIOUS ORDER
ORIGINAL TITLE   PLACE
                                INSTITUTION
                                DIOCESE

NON-TEXTUAL (complementary data)

FOLIOS OF TEXT
BIBLIOGRAPHICAL REFERENCES
DECORATION
HERALDRY
MUSIC
POETRY
AD LIBITUM

REFERENCES

Beaud, M.-J., Fossier, L. (1977). *Guide pour l'élaboration d'une notice de manuscrit*. Paris: I.R.H.T. Bibliographies, colloques, travaux préparatoires.

Beaud, M.-J., Guillaumont, A., Minel, J.-L. (1983). A Médiéval manuscript database. In R.F. Allen (Ed.), *The International Conference on Data Bases in the Humanities and Social Sciences*, Rutgers—The State University of New Jersey (pp. 22-29). Osprey, Florida: Paradigm Press.

Boehm, D., Naud, A. (1985). *Interface S.A.S. –ADABAS*. Orsay: Documentation C.I.R.C.E.

Bourlet, C., Fossier, L., Guillaumont, A., Minel, J-L. (1985). *Projet de construction d'un système expert dans le domaine historique*. Paris: Documentation IRHT.

Folkerts, M. and Kühne, A. *The Use of Computers in Cataloging Medieval and Renaissance Manuscripts*. Papers from the International Workshop in Munich, 10-12 August 1989 (1990). In *Algorismus*, Studien zur Geschichte der Mathematik und der Naturwissenschaften, ed. M. Folkerts. München: Institut für Geschichte der Naturwissenschaften.

Fossier, L. (1980). *Guide du lecteur de l'Institut de Recherche et d'Histoire des Textes*. Paris: IRHT.

————— (1985). Manuscrit médiéval et informatique. Problèmes de constitution d'une base de données. *Revue, Informatique et Statistique dans les Sciences Humaines, 21*, pp. 109-122.

————— (1988). *Banque de données du manuscrit médiéval à l'Institut de Recherche et d'Histoire des Textes*. Paris: IRHT, unpublished.

Fossier, L. and Beaud, M.-J. (1986). Introducing the Institut de Recherche et d'Histoire des Textes (C.N.R.S.): Medieval Book and Computer. *Computers and the Humanities, 20*, pp. 267-268.

Fossier, L. and Courtemanche (1987). La base de données sur le manuscrit médiéval Medium de l'IRHT: réflexion sur les problèmes de protection juridique et de valorisation des données. "Table Ronde: Standardisation et échanges des bases de données historiques." Paris: CNRS, to be published.

Guillaumont, A. and Minel, J.-L. (1984). MEDIUM, base de données sur le manuscrit médiéval. In *Census. Automatic Processing of Art History Data and Documents, 1*, pp. 419-435. Pisa.

————— (1986). MEDIUM, Realities and projects. *Computers and the Humanities, 20*, pp.269-271.

————— (1987). MEDIUM, conception, réalisation et exploitation d'une base de données. In *Polata Knigopisnaja*, 17-18, Nimègue, pp. 60-65.

————— (1990). MEDIUM, base de données sur le manuscrit médiéval. Un exemple d'application en histoire des sciences. In *The Use of Computers in Cataloging*, pp. 57-64.

Stevens, W.M. (1990). Problems and proposals for machine readable manuscript catalogues. In *The Use of Computers in Cataloging*, pp. 149-175.

Central Cataloguing
of Medieval Manuscripts
in the Eastern
Provinces of Germany

Renate Schipke

SUMMARY. Efforts to provide descriptions of the many collections of Latin manuscripts in the Eastern Provinces of Germany were renewed in 1972 by establishing the Central Inventory of Medieval Manuscripts (Zentralinventar mittelalterlicher Handschriften bis 1500 in den Sammlungen der DDR), called *ZIH*. The *ZIH* will give a brief description of each manuscript in twelve categories, including foliation, author, title, incipit, and explicit of each work, as the "first level" of identification. From this will be developed several registers for different types of information. One of these is the Central Registry of Incipits (Zentrales Initienregister, or *ZIR*) which is accessible by computer at the Deutsches Staatsbibliothek, Berlin. The *ZIR* has created its own computer programme and provided ten categories of information about each tract. It will retrieve the data by means of the characters of the incipit given by the manuscript as well as by means of a pseudo incipit which is efficient for searching.

Manuscripts are scattered in many libraries and archives throughout the former German Democratic Republic, now part of the reunified German nation. Some of the manuscripts are known to scholars through published catalogues, but most are hidden in various collections and are often imperfectly catalogued. If they are known to the current world of scholarship it may be almost by accident, and it

Frau Dr. Renate Schipke is Librarian in the Manuscript Department and Literary Archive of the Deutsche Staatsbibliothek in Berlin. She has published several manuscript catalogues and other medieval studies.

is highly probable that many significant manuscripts are completely unknown to those who need them to explain past events and culture. This is a very difficult situation especially for scholars beginning to do their work without some indication of where their sources might be and what documents the manuscripts may contain. Thus many efforts have been made to produce catalogues of medieval manuscripts.

A catalogue of manuscripts in Germany was begun in the 1920s, entitled *Verzeichnis der Handschriften im Preußischen Staate*, and two volumes were published in 1938 and 1942.[1] Even limited cataloguing activities were interrupted of course by World War II. In 1952 however the Commission for Manuscripts and Incunabula was founded to continue the work of cataloguing within the newly formed German Democratic Republic or DDR. But in spite of the greatest efforts by some scholars to carry forward the cataloguing of manuscripts, there were not many successes. The situation became better in 1972 when the Deutsche Staatsbibliothek in East Berlin undertook to organise a Central Inventory of Medieval Manuscripts (Zentralinventar mittelalterlicher Handschriften bis 1500 in den Sammlungen der DDR), called *ZIH*. It is administered by the Department of Manuscripts of that library and is intended at first to account for all Latin manuscripts within the country. It was decided that the *ZIH* should be a limited and accessible inventory instead of a fully descriptive catalogue for two reasons: staff and time. Only a few workers could be engaged, and for a long time there was only a single person assigned to the task; moreover, it was expected that an inventory with concise data could be brought to a practical conclusion within a limited time, whereas a full cataloguing project could not be completed within a forseeable period.

Manuscripts in the Latin language are the focal point of the *ZIH*, and there are about 10,000 to 12,000 items in collections of the DDR. These have been relatively neglected, in contrast with manuscripts in the German language. In the Archive of Manuscripts of the Academy of Sciences in Berlin are catalogue descriptions of about 19,000 German manuscripts written up to A.D. 1500; and based upon this descriptive material are three published catalogues (Menhardt, 1960-61; Pensel, 1977, 1986). Thus a comprehensive inventory of Latin manuscripts was needed.

The structure of *ZIH* consists of a basic alphabetical catalogue of the locations of collections and of their manuscripts. A schema of twelve categories of information was developed for the manuscript descriptions to be included:

1. City, name of library, and shelfmark
2. Former shelfmarks
3. Material of the codex
4. Number of leaves
5. Format size in centimeters
6. Location
7. Scribe
8. Century or date of composition
9. Decoration
10. Provenance
11. Selected literature about the manuscript
12. Contents.

By this format a model is provided by which other librarians and scholars could make inventories for each separate collection. From these beginnings they could also develop descriptive catalogues when staff and time were available. We also intended to use computer technology with the Central Inventory in order to produce several types of indices for the use of individual scholars who are interested in particular topics.

Category 12 is the focal point of information about the contents of a manuscript; within it the contents are classified according to foliation, author and title or only title (if an author is unknown), incipit and explicit. This schema for category 12 includes the most important information about any manuscript at "First Level."[2]

For the cataloguing of material on different levels of complexity, we also developed special rules which may be used for more extensive descriptions; for short description of a repertory; and for descriptions of early modern manuscripts, bequests, autographs, and printed books with handwritten notes (*Regeln*, 1983). Catalogues of single collections in accord with these rules for the Evangelischer Predigerseminar Wittenberg, the Schneeberger Collection of the Sächsische Landesbibliothek Dresden, and the Stadtbibliothek Dessau are printed in the Series of Inventories of Manuscripts published by the Department of Manuscripts of the Deutsche Staatsbibliothek, Berlin.[3] Each new catalogue includes several indices. The registers or indices for separate collections of Latin manuscripts in an archive or library as well as registers for several collections together are very important for scholars. The *ZIH* should be able to produce them.

Our schema of categories is readily adaptable for use with a computer, and this has allowed us to begin the development of a programme for the Central Registry of Incipits or Zentrales Initienregister, called *ZIR*. At the beginning of 1988 in collaboration with the Computer Department of the Deutsche Staatsbibliothek, a computer programme was created which will allow us to prepare a database containing the incipits of Latin tracts contained in medieval manuscripts which are preserved in East German libraries. Data recorded with each incipit of the *ZIR* are organised as follows:

1. Incipit
2. Author
3. Title
4. Addition to title
5. Other additions to title
6. City
7. Key number
8. Library
9. Shelfmark
10. Foliation of the tract.

Sources for the *ZIR-Project* are the modern printed catalogues or our own descriptions of manuscripts. Card indexes are produced both for recording data and for correcting them. By July 1989, 2,696 incipits were contained in the *ZIR* database from 3,093 locations in manuscripts, entered by collaborator of the *ZIH*. There are estimated to be 6,000 incipits of works in the Latin manuscripts of the Deutsche Staatsbibliothek to be entered in the *ZIR* database, and we expect this part to appear as a printed book.

The next stage will be to enter further incipits into its database, for example: incipits from the famous manuscripts in the Collection

Amploniana in Erfurt which contain many medieval scientific texts, especially from the fourteenth and fifteenth centuries. At the present time the Erfurt catalogues do not provide scholars with an index of incipits, but they are already available in the *ZIH*. These incipits will be transferred to the *ZIR* database and published. As further inventory data becomes available in *ZIH*, incipits and related content information from its Category 12 may be transferred into the *ZIR* database. Furthermore, we wish also to develop a central register of authors and titles.

At present retrieval enquiries may be made only by incipit, not by authors or titles. Some scholars depend upon a search for an author's name. In order to solve the problem posed by the variations of spelling for names of medieval authors, the creators and the users of the *ZIH* and the *ZIR* require ancillary tools, especially alphabetical listings of authors' names in all forms of occurrence. A normalised list for these databases is useful for determining correct form of each name when entering the data, and this also allows for easy retrieval. Of course this applies equally to the titles of tracts.

Data search by means of incipit however makes it possible to overcome difficulties of trying to identify a medieval text in which the author's name or the title appears in an unusual form, or in which the author's name and the title are lacking. Thus repertories of incipits are very important for scholars. Most lists of incipits in published catalogues are quite limited in value; usually such a list will contain an incipit only once and this may be in a unique form as found in a single manuscript, without any further information being provided. Thus the scholar is usually forced to use a great number of manuscript catalogues with inconsistent indices and incipit lists, or to seek out many manuscripts themselves in distant locations before being able to identify the proper author or title.

The *ZIR-Project* intends to assist the scholars who face such problems by producing a repertory of incipits which also contains as much data about authors and titles as possible. We think that it offers a new possibility for simplifying the work of scholars, as others have recognised (Bratley, Hamesse, 1990).[4] In order to simplify enquiries, we have also arranged for a pseudo incipit to be formed. The pseudo incipit takes the first letter of every word of the actual incipit up to a total of 20 letters. Our experience with the incipits and pseudo incipits has shown that a sequence of three letters may often be enough for retrieving data about a text which the user is seeking.

Data input of descriptions and data output for retrieval requests or for corrections and additions are realised at a local terminal in a relational database management system IDAS using programme C language, together with CQL. For technical realisation of the *ZIR* we use SM 4-20 hardware with 256 KB and UNIX version 7 with 2.5 MB or UNIX BSD 2.9 with 20 MB.[5]

Several other projects were presented during the Symposium on "Computer Programmes for Medieval and Renaissance Manuscript Sources" at the International Congress of History of Science (Hamburg and Munich, 5-7 August 1989) and during the "Workshop on the Use of Computers" (Deutsches Museum, Munich, 10-12 August 1989). In comparison with them, it is the primary task of the *ZIR* at the Deutsche Staatsbibliothek to produce a central inventory of medieval Latin manuscripts which are located in archives and libraries of the eastern provinces of Germany. Therefore scholars responsible for and interested in these collections should prepare new descriptions of uncatalogued manuscripts for the *ZIH*, which will allow us to transfer their incipits into the *ZIR* database. The *ZIR-Project* will then be able to respond to enquiries by providing convenient and readable information about the texts in those manuscripts for scholarly analysis.[6]

NOTES

1. Breslau: Universitätsbibliothek, 1938; Graz: Universitätsbibliothek, 1942.

2. During 1974-1976 we attempted to create computer programmes which would produce several registers of data in this way. Because of the extensive data required for the description of a manuscript we were not able to realise the project at that time.

3. *ZIH Handschrifteninventare*, Nr. 7: *Die Handschriften des Evangelischen Predigerseminars Wittenberg* (1984); Nr. 8: *Die mittelalterlichen Schneeberger Handschriften der Sächsischen Landesbibliothek Dresden* (1986); Nr. 10: *Die lateinischen Handschriften der Stadtbibliothek Dessau* (1986).

4. We have recently learned of the Repertoire des incipits des manuscrits led by Paul Bratley (Montréal) and Jacqueline Hamesse (Louvain-la-Neuve) and based at the Institut d'études médiévales, Université catholique de Louvain, Bel-

gium (Bratley, Hamesse, 1990). Many thanks to Professor Stevens, University of Winnipeg, for this information in his letter of June 30, 1989.

5. Since April 1990 data input, output, and so forth are realised in a relational database management system Daba 32 (i.e., INGRES, from University of California at Berkeley) using programme C language together with EQL, and we use K1840-ROBOTON hardware (VAX-compatible).

6. An earlier version of this paper was read by Dr. A. Kühne in my behalf to the International Congress of History of Science on 5 August 1989 in Hamburg. I was able to present another version for the International Workshop in München, 10-12 August, "Die zentrale Katalogisierung mittelalterlicher Handschriften in der DDR," which was published in *The Use of computers in cataloging* (1990), pp. 81-90. I wish to thank Professor W. Stevens for advice on further revisions and for his assistance with the English translation.

REFERENCES

Bratley, P., Hamesse, J. (1990). The computerisation of manuscript incipits. In *Computers in Literary and Linguistic Research, Actes de la XVe Conference Internationale, Jerusalem, 5-9 Juin 1988* (ed. Y. Choueka), pp. 138-145. Paris, Genéve: Champion-Slatkine.

Menhardt, H. (1960-1961). *Verzeichnis der deutschen Handschriften der österreichischen Nationalbibliothek*, 3 Bände. Berlin. (Veröffentlichungen des Instituts für deutsche Sprache und Literatur, 13.1-3).

Pensel, F. (1977). *Verzeichnis der altdeutschen Handschriften der Stadtbibliothek Dessau*. Berlin. (Deutsche Texte des Mittelalters, 70.1).

———— (1986). *Verzeichnis der altdeutschen Handschriften der Universitätsbibliothek Jena*. Berlin. (Deutsche Texte des Mittelalters, 70.2).

———— (1986). *Verzeichnis der altdeutschen Handschriften der Universitätsbibliothek Leipzig*. Berlin. (Deutsche Texte des Mittelalters, 70.2); im Druck.

Schipke, R. (1983). Die Katalogisierung mittelalterlicher Handschriften in der Deutschen Demokratischen Republik. Ein Arbeitsbericht. *Scriptorium*, *37*, 2, pp. 275-285.

Schipke, R. with Hoffmann, G. (1981). Zentrale Katalogisierung mittelalterlicher Handschriften in der DDR. Versuch einer datenverarbeitungsgerechten Aufbereitung. *Studien zum Buch- und Bibliothekswesen*, *1*, pp. 42-53. Leipzig.

Winter, U., Schipke R., Teitge H.-E. (1983). *Regeln für die Katalogisierung von Handschriften*. Berlin. Im Auftrag der Deutschen Staatsbibliothek.

APPENDIX I

Manuscripts from the following collections and libraries were included by 1989 in the Central Inventory of Medieval Manuscripts (Zentralinventar mittelalterlicher Handschriften bis 1500 in den Sammlungen der DDR), called *ZIH*.

	Handschriften und Fragmente
Angermünde, Stadtmuseum	5
Bautzen, Stadt- und Kreisbibliothek	14
Berlin, Deutsche Staatsbibliothek	838
Berlin, St. Marien Bibliothek	6
Barth, Kirchenbibliothek	9
Brandenburg/Havel, Domstiftsarchiv	6
Dessau, Stadtbibliothek	51
Dresden, Sächsische Landesbibliothek	418
Eisleben, Turmbibliothek St. Andreas	15
Erfurt, Wissenschaftliche Allgemeinbibliothek	950
Frankfurt/Oder, St. Marien Bibliothek	6
Freiberg/Sachsen, Bibliothek der Erweiterten Oberschule "Geschwister Scholl"	2
Fürstenwalde, Ehemalige Dombibliothek	6
Görlitz, Bibliothek der Oberlausitzischen Gesellschaft der Wissenschaften	3
Gotha, Forschungsbibliothek	133
Greifswald, Bibliothek des Geistlichen Ministeriums	1
Halle/Saale, Hauptbibliothek der Franckische Stiftungen	12
Halle/Saale, Marienbibliothek	14
Halle/Saale, Universitäts- und Landesbibliothek	384
Havelberg, Domarchiv	1
Jena, Universitätsbibliothek	6
Leipzig, Deutsche Bücherei	9
Leipzig, Universitätsbibliothek	36
Mülhausen, Kreisarchiv	43
Naumburg, Katechetisches Oberseminar	1
Neuruppin, Kirchenbibliothek	3

Perleberg, Superintendentur (Pfarrbibliothek Uenze)   1
Quedlinburg, St. Nicolai-Kirche   2
Ruhlsdorf (bei Bernau), Pfarrarchiv   1
Salzwedel, St. Katharinen-Kirche   1
Sangerhausen, St. Ulrichs-Kirche   2
Schwerin, Bibliothek des Oberkirchenrates   4
Wittenberg, Evangelisches Predigerseminar   12
Wittenberg, Staatliche Lutherhalle   8
Wittstock, Ephoralarchiv   11
Zerbst, Stadtbibliothek   13
Zittau, Stadt- und Kreisbibliothek "Christian Weise"   15
Zwickau, Ratsschulbibliothek   77

APPENDIX II

Selected incipit files from the Central Registry of Incipits (Zentrales Initienregister), called *ZIR*.

Ad primum sic proceditur videtur quod homini non conveniat
     Thomas de Aquino: Summa theologica, pars II, 1
     BERLIN, *St. Marien-Bibliothek*, Hs.3,2, f.2ra, 2rb. GOTHA,
         Forschungsbibliothek, Memb.I 53, f.17va; Chart.B 123,
         f.205r. MÜHLHAUSEN, *Kreis-archiv*, 60/15, f.201r
Adolescens qui meretricis amore tenebatur
     Terentius: Hecyra
     BERLIN, *Deutsche Staatsbibliothek*, Hamilton 620, f.81r;
         Hamilton 622, f.69r; Hamilton 624, f.91v; Phill.1789, f.7r;
         Phill.2087, f.12v
Aequivoca dicuntur quorum solum
     Aristoteles: Categoriae (lat.)
     DESSAU, *Stadtbibliothek*, Georg Hs.209 Quart., f.5r. ER-
         FURT, *Wiss. Allgemeinbibliothek*, Amplon. Fol.39, f.9v;
         Amplon.Quart.20, f.6r; Amplon.Quart. 267, f.7r; Amplon.
         Quart.271, f.101v; Amplon. Quart. 340, f.9r. HALLE/Sa.,
         Univ.- u. Landesbibliothek, YG Fol.3, f.8va
Exaltent eum in ecclesia plebis . . . (Ps 106, 32). In verbis istis ad
         honorem beati Petri tria spiritualiter
     Sermones de confessoribus

BERLIN, *Deutsche Staatsbibliothek*, Phill. 1753, f.131rb. *St. Marien-Bibliothek*, Hs.3,1, f.12va. EISLEBEN, *Turmbibliothek St. Andreas*, 961, f.242vb

Flores grammaticae propono scribere Christe

Ludolphus de Luckowe: Flores grammaticae

BERLIN, *Deutsche Staatsbibliothek*, Hamilton 63, f.14r; Phill.2002, f.243vb. ERFURT, *Wiss. Allgemeinbibliothek*, Amplon.Quart 47, f.38r; Amplon.48, f.1r; Amplon.Quart 70, f.1r. GOTHA, *Forschungsbibliothek*, Memb.II 130, f.1r

Gregorius episcopus servus servorum Dei dilectis filiis doctoribus et scolaribus Parisiis commorantibus salutem et apostolicam benedictionem. Rex pacificus

Gregorius papa IX: Decretales (cum glossis)

BERLIN, *Deutsche Staatsbibliothek*, Phill.1803, f.12v. HALLE/Sa., *Univ.- und Landesbibliothek*, Ye Fol.32, f.1ra; Ye Fol.40, f.1ra; Ye Fol.47, f.4ra. ZWICKAU, *Ratsschulbibliothek*, XIII,4,5, f.2ra

Humano capiti cervicem pictor equinam

Horatius: Carmina

BERLIN, *Deutsche Staatsbibliothek*, Hamilton 228, f.17r; Hamilton 333, f.244v; Hamilton 334, f.51vb. DESSAU, *Stadtbibliothek*, HB Hs.1, f.23v; HB Hs.2, f.23r. DRESDEN, *Sächsische Landesbibliothek*, D 140, f.2r. ZWICKAU, *Ratsschulbibliothek*, XIII,2,4, f.272r

In Persida civitate Diospoli sancti Georgii martyris cuius gesta

(S. Georgius): Passio S. Georgii

BERLIN, *Deutsche Staatsbibliothek*, Hamilton 643, f.12vb; Phill.1769, f.247ra. ZITTAU, *Christian-Weise-Bibliothek*, A 303, f.171rb

Iussioni tuae sancte frater Aureli tanto devotius obtemperare

Augustinus: De opere monachorum

BERLIN, *Deutsche Staatsbibliothek*, Phill.1817, f.12v; Phill.2001, f.57ra. JENA, *Universitätsbibliothek*, El. quart.7, f.97r. HALLE/Sa., *Univ.- und Landesbibliothek*, QU.Cod.123, f.170r. ZWICKAU, *Ratsschulbibliothek*, V, f.17r

Lucas Syrus natione Antiochensis, arte medicus, discipulus apostolorum

Ps-Hieronymus: Prologus in evangelium Lucae

BERLIN, *Deutsche Staatsbibliothek*, Phill.1644 (II), f.168rb; Phill.1649, f.1ra; Phill.2001, f.362ra; Phill.2003, f.23rb. DESSAU, *Stadtbibliothek*, Georg.Hs.1, f.286ra; Georg.Hs. 4 Quart., f.51r. GOTHA, *Forschungsbibliothek*, Memb.I 18, f.117vb; Memb.I 20, f.59v; Memb.I 22, f.100v; Memb. II 14, f.86r; Memb.II 88, f.73r. HALLE/Sa., *Marienbibliothek*, 6, f.239vb. *Univ.- und Landesbibliothek*, Stolb.-Wernig.Za 12, f.375 vb. LEIPZIG, *Universitätsbibliothek*, 143, f.56r. WITTENBERG, *Bibl. des Evang. Priesterseminars*, A VI 3, f.406r. *Lutherhalle*, S 165/1362, f.398va. WITTSTOCK, *Ephoralarchiv*, o.S., f.226va

Meditatio est frequens cogitatio

Hugo de Sancto Victore: De meditatione

BERLIN, *Deutsche Staatsbibliothek*, Diez B Sant.32, f.14r; Diez C, f.143va; Hamilton 93, f.59ra; Hamilton 393, f.201v; Phill.1403, f.12vb; Phill.1863, f. 27r; Phill.1889, f.293v. EISLEBEN, *Turmbibliothek St. Andreas*, 960, f.109v. ERFURT, *Wiss. Allgemeinbibl.*, Amplon. Quart.145, f.101v; Amplon.Quart.147, f.113r. LEIPZIG, *Universitätsbibliothek*, Theol.395, f.34v

Qui fit Maecenas ut nemo quam sibi sortem

Horatius: Sermones

BERLIN, *Deutsche Staatsbibliothek*, Hamilton 332, f.66. DESSAU, *Stadtbibliothek*, HB Hs.1, f.62r; HB Hs. 2, f.28r; HB Hs.7, f.9v

Regressus ad nos filius meus Adeodatus sedis nostrae diaconus

Leo papa I: Epistolae (Ep. 159 ad Nicetam)

BERLIN, *Deutsche Staatsbibliothek*, Phill.1741, f.144v; Phill.1743, f.228vb; Phill.1744, f.96vb. GOTHA, *Forschungsbibliothek*, Memb.I 120, f.61v; Memb.II 12, f.213va

Si veraceus fidelesque amici cuiuspiam aegroti curam diligentius agant

Johannes Gerson: De arte moriendi

BERLIN, *Deutsche Staatsbibliothek*, Theol.lat. quart.207,

f.350r. DRESDEN, *Sächsische Landesbibliothek*, App. 2293, f.87r

Tres leo naturas et tres habet inde figuras
Theobaldus: (Commentarius in physiologum)
ERFURT, *Wiss. Allgemeinbibliothek*, Amplon.Quart. 317, f.107r. GOTHA, *Forschungsbibliothek*, Memb.II 120, f.51v. HALLE/Sa., *Archiv der Franckeschen Stiftungen*, 61 F 15, f.62v

Usque modo si quam me scriptitasse iussistis, aut invitus aut nulla-tenus
Bernhardus Claraevallensis: Apologia ad Guilelmum
BERLIN, *Deutsche Staatsbibliothek*, Diez B Sant.5, f.3ra; Diez B Sant.62, f.62, f.122r; Diez C Quart.15, f.27vb; Hamilton 636, f.14r; Hamilton 712, f.253vb; Lat.Fol.698, f.252v; Phill.1969, f.20vb, f.93ra; Phill.1996, f.253r. ER-FURT, *Wiss. Allgemeinbibliothek*, Amplon.Quart.29, f.13va; Amplon.Oct.212, f.5r. GOTHA, *Forschungsbibliothek*, Chart.A 17, f.5r, f.12v; Chart.B 1253, f.233vb; Memb.I 115, f.1r; Memb.II 25, f.35r

Visio Isaiae filii Amos . . . Subintelligentur in primis haec est, ut ita sit integer sensus
Hervaeus Burgidolensis: Commentaria in Isaiam
BERLIN, *Deutsche Staatsbibliothek*, Phill.1658, f.4ra

A Manuscript Databank
for the History of Mathematics
in Medieval and Renaissance Europe

Andreas Kühne

SUMMARY. Of the one million Latin manuscripts which survive, about 5000 contain mathematical texts in Latin and European languages. With EDV they have been described in the International Computer Catalogue of Medieval Scientific Manuscripts, called ICC MSM, under direction of Professor Menso Folkerts at the University of Munich. Full descriptions rather than texts are entered in a PC-AT with 110 MB memory. The descriptions are based upon analyses already published or those prepared for internal use of the libraries. The encoding system was developed from current cataloguing standards and the *Richtlinien zur Handschriftenkatalogisierung* der DFG (1985) for very detailed information.

Enquiries to the ICC MSM data base allows search of Location, Shelfmark, Date, Language, Author, Translator, Commentator, Scribe, Title, and Incipit. Among the first results has been discovery of further copies of known and of heretofore unknown mathematical texts.

At the onset of every new project the use of computers in the historical sciences poses the question as to whether databanks can serve only in preparation for publication or whether they effectively replace these publications altogether. Especially in work with manuscript catalogues and regardless of whether the manuscripts con-

---

Dr. Andreas Kühne was Computer Technician and Archivist for the Deutsche Akademie der Naturforscher Leopoldina (Halle/Saale) and Co-editor of the *Acta Historica Leopoldina*. He is now Technical and Organising Head of the ICC MSM in the Institut für Geschichte der Naturwissenschaften der Universität München.

cerned deal with liturgical, literary, or as in this case mathematical themes, this question cannot be answered in a general manner because the high degree of abstraction which the input of manuscript descriptions entails reduces the contextual redundancy and thus the readability of a resulting catalogue.

Hence the International Computer Catalogue of Medieval Scientific Manuscripts is not intended to replace existing catalogues (Folkerts, 1984, pp. 36-41, 1990). The ICC MSM was developed by a team under the direction of Professor Menso Folkerts at the Institute for the History of Science at the University of Munich. It is designed to facilitate the use of published catalogues and library inventories of manuscript collections. The problem of a reduced scope of association in interpreting catalogue entries is in this case only marginally relevant, since the project of a databank for medieval and particularly mathematical manuscripts was conceived primarily as a retrieval system. But due to the complexity of the input data, the path which M. Thaller (1989, p. 220) has proposed remains viable; that is, instruments can be created to make possible "further publications in the form of static excerpts of a dynamic representation."

DEFINITION OF THE DATA BASE

Boundaries of Language and Time: In accordance with the project's conception for the construction of a databank for the history of medieval mathematics, details of texts in Latin and in the vernacular languages (French, English, Catalan, Provençal etc.) were put into the databank in the appropriate form. While not wishing to define the limits of the middle ages, the years 500 and 1500 were deemed appropriate historical boundaries. Manuscripts written between these dates have been recorded as completely as possible, but the boundaries have sometimes been exceeded as far as the 19th century in order to obviate the necessity of a renewed evaluation of published catalogues with respect to more recent manuscripts. An analysis of special "lists of Nachlasses" has not yet been undertaken.

Subject matter: At first, neither texts dealing with the computation of calendars (computus) nor those concerning logic, physics and astronomy were to be included in the databank. However in listing the data it was useful to include texts to the extent that they were described in existing catalogues. Time-consuming decisions were thereby avoided, for example whether or not treatises on the theory of motion, on proportions and on astronomical and geodetic instruments should be considered. Mathematical texts which comprised parts of non-mathematical encyclopedias or other collections could be included only if they appeared as independent and explicitly defined sections of the larger text. In these cases lesser pieces such as multiplication- and number-tables or comments on the number-value of letters were taken into consideration. In borderline cases manuscripts were generally included rather than ignored. In this way a data base has emerged which remains flexible at its boundaries but which exhibits a reasonable degree of completeness at its core of specifically mathematical manuscripts.

COMPILATION OF THE MANUSCRIPTS

An important requirement in the compilation of data was that the data created could be transformed easily into pure ASCII values in order to allow for an exchange of information between databanks. This requirement was met by using the text processing system Nota Bene (Version 3.0). The data to be stored had to be clearly categorized and presented so that recourse to the primary source or microfilm copies is not normally necessary.
The data originates from three sources:

1. analysis of published manuscript catalogues or catalogues designed solely for internal library use;
2. analysis of scientific literature which either describes in detail or edits the manuscripts;
3. examination of the original manuscript or its microfilm copy.

The descriptions of the manuscripts included in the data base verified so that for example some of the erroneous incipits of Thorndike/ Kibre (1963) could be corrected. Great care was taken in establishing the past and present location and catalogue-number of the manuscripts, especially when secondary sources contradicted one another. Warren Van Egmond developed a specific encoding system based upon the data structure of the manuscript descriptions at the Benjamin Data Bank in Dunellen, New Jersey (Hahn et alii 1983), the guidelines of the Deutsche Forschungsgemeinschaft for cataloging manuscripts (Richtlinien, 1985), and his own research (Van Egmond, 1986). The system is particularly suitable for the range and content of medieval and renaissance manuscripts. It consists of a series of two-digit reference numbers, some of which contain information concerning the entire manuscript while others refer to separate sections of the codex and can be repeated if desired. Furthermore by attaching an additional two-digit reference number, the origin of the information can be given.

Fields 01, 02, . . . 99 of the encoding system contain all categories necessary for a bibliographical description of the manuscript. For example the language of a manuscript (Latin, German, English etc.) is given in field 14.NN. The term .NN refers to the source of information used — for example .01 (Zinner, 1925); .02 (Kristeller, 1960). Full bibliographical reference is given in category 44 (catalogue name); e.g., 44.01 (Zinner, Ernst. *Verzeichnis der astronomischen Handschriften des deutschen Kulturgebietes*. München: 1925). In this manner a broad bibliography of bibliographies of medieval scientific manuscripts was created as a by-product of the compilation procedure.

Analysis of Contents

The standardization of the input data was linked to the previously mentioned verification of the existing catalogue data. Aside from this standardization of input data, further analysis such as classifying, indexing or referencing was not undertaken due to the sheer volume of material. A suitable content analysis would be time consuming and require expertise of both a historian of science and a paleographer. Computer-aided determination of content (i.e., an indexing of the incipits and titles) using existing indexing programs like GOLEM, is not very promising because the incipits and titles of medieval manuscripts do not always reflect the content of the works.

Retrievable fields: Not all of the data indicating text content has been labelled so that they become accessible to search procedures. But twenty-one descriptive categories can be accessed in a search procedure:

01 – country
02 – city
03 – library
05 – current library number
06 – previous catalogue number
08 – short title
11 – century
12 – precise date of the manuscript
14 – language
15 – subject matter of the manuscript
16 – finer subject division
31 – name or sign of scribe
52 – author (standard spelling)
53 – author (spelling in the manuscript)
54 – short title (standard spelling)
55 – short title (spelling in the manuscript)
56 – additional names
57 – names or signs of scribes of individual portions of the codex
61 – full title
64 – incipit
65 – second incipit

Search Procedure

By May 1990 the data base of ICC MSM has grown to 60 MB, and it is located on an IBM-compatible PC/AT with a 110 MB hard disk. Data which has been freshly encoded or which has been made available by exchange with other institutions, such as the Benjamin Catalogue, is input by means of 360 kB or 1.2 MB diskettes. The consolidation of all input data in the Information Retrieval System "Aktor 1.7" makes possible an on-line search of all indexed fields. Within the "Aktor" system a search is possible either by direct input of a string of reference terms or by input of a string of reference numbers. Up to 30 such numbers and/or terms can be linked together.

The search, which is formulated in terms of boolean algebra, is conducted with the logical operators AND, OR, and NAND. As with the majority of existing retrieval systems, search commands in the "Aktor" system must be formulated in logical statements. Searches for names of authors should take all variations in spelling into consideration. The various spellings can be taken from the index of names.

STATISTICAL EXAMINATION
OF THE ENTIRE BASE

Methodological considerations: After compilation of manuscript descriptions has been completed, further relationships can be investigated which would remain inaccessible to analysis by conventional bibliographic means. If the basic data is sufficiently standardized, it is possible to use evaluation procedures developed for very different statistical applications. The goal of statistical work on the data stored in the ICC MSM catalogue is the acquisition of new information by extracting, ordering, evaluating and condensing the retrieved data. The goal is not to gain new information concerning the data base but rather to acquire meaningful answers to specific historical questions.

The size of the data base: At present the entire ICC MSM databank contains descriptions of 9175 codices from the period between 500 and 1500. These codices consist of 49919 sections; that is, every codex on average is made up of 5.4 different parts which are partly or wholly distinct. The total number of parts in the codices is higher of course since only mathematical sections were incorporated in the databank from large liturgical and ecclesiastical codices. Seven thousand four hundred sixty-two manuscripts comprise the databank's core and are of particular importance for research on the middle ages and renaissance.

Language distribution: Although the exact number of medieval mathematical manuscripts is unknown, valid statements concerning the distribution of Latin and vernacular texts can be made because the same percentage rates show up in different samplings of the manuscript data base. Of the 7462 manuscripts, 5840 were written in Latin and 1225 in the vernacular languages (16.4%) with 397 in

Greek. The vernacular manuscripts are divided among the following languages.

Italian	=	377
German	=	346
French	=	231
English	=	126
Spanish	=	58
Catalan	=	48
Dutch	=	17
Provençal	=	13
Bohemian	=	7

The proportion of German-language manuscripts appears to be somewhat over-represented, since to date the manuscripts of no other country within the data base have been so thoroughly incorporated than German manuscripts.

Historical distribution: Using dates, authors, languages, and themes as starting points, statistically significant statements concerning evidence of the entire data base may be made. Only isolated vernacular mathematical texts were known in the period from ninth to twelfth centuries, but a decline of the number of technical manuscripts surviving in the twelfth century reported by Klemm (1982) finds correlation in the mathematical manuscripts, relative to those known from the eleventh. A significant number of non-Latin technical and mathematical texts appeared first in the thirteenth century, confirming the estimates of Eis (1962) and Folkerts (1988). But our evidence shows an exponential growth between 1300 and 1500 in both Latin and vernacular texts and a decline thereafter. Italian texts reveal the opposite pattern: earlier decline and then growth in the sixteenth century, as previously affirmed by Withrow (1988). Details and illustrations of these results have been reported by Kühne (1990).

Treatment of proper names: From the perspective of prosopography the ICC MSM databank also represents a useful research aid in conjunction with conventional reference materials, for example *Die deutsche Literatur des Mittelalters, Verfasserlexikon* (1938). For medieval German proper names the computer dictionary *WSF*

(Geuenich, 1988) is a useful instrument for this purpose. As with all other information describing manuscripts, proper names were entered into the ICC MSM data base in the form in which they appeared in the description or the manuscript itself. In those cases in which a sufficient number of references was made it is possible to determine a standardized spelling, that spelling was entered in category 53. The index of names of the manuscript catalogue of the Institut de Recherche et d'Histoire des Textes (Liste des auteurs, 1988) was used as a primary source. If the title, offices or surnames (cognomen) of the author were known, these were listed after the proper name. If several names were used (for example Latin and vernacular names) these variation were entered separately. The index of names automatically contains numerous spellings of author's names as a result of the internal program "Prepare" which labels all names in their various spellings. Cross references to the standardized spelling of the name—in so far as such a standardization exists—can be introduced into the index only as part of a second operation. However this supplementary operation is simplified by the wide range of search possibilities in the index. For example all names contained in the incipits or manuscript titles can be selected and compared. At present the only possibility for statistical evaluation lies in the determination of the absolute and relative frequency of the appearance of names within the index.

A distinction is made between three groups of names in the sorting of input categories: Authors, Scribes, and Others.

Authors: An author is identified as any person who is related to the text as a consequence of authorship, of a prologue, a commentary, an interpretation, a translation, or editing, publishing, or excerpting. The name is entered under category "52" (standardized spelling) and/or "53" (spelling in the manuscript).

Scribes: The name or signs of the scribes are entered under category "31" for the entire manuscript and/or category "57" for individual sections of the codex. If there are several scribes the names or signs are listed in chronological order along with the folio numbers; for example alpha (1r - 26r); beta (27r - 29r).

Others: Category "56" encompasses the names of all other persons who are formally connected with the text—for example the dedicator, dedicatee, owner, or the teacher of the author etc.—most usually as a result of ownership. The current omission of morphological analysis was the result of pragmatic and not conceptual considerations. Because the index of names can be used as a separate file, independent of other sections of the index, the subsequent implementation of morphological analysis is possible.

Distribution analysis of authors: Analysis of the index of names in the ICC MSM databank led to the following list of authors. The ranking of the authors on the list depends on the frequency with which they are cited. In order to compile more precise information, a further analysis will have to be undertaken after the data input has been completed.

> Aristotle (848 cit.)
> Euclid (357 cit.)
> Boethius (325 cit.)
> Messehala (309 cit.)
> Ptolemy (237 cit.)
> Johannes Hispalensis (185 cit.)
> Albertus Magnus (173 cit.)
> Thabit ben Qurra (171 cit.)
> Alexander de Villa Dei (157 cit.)
> Raimundus Lullus (119 cit.)
> Beda (115 cit.)
> Haly Abenragel (106 cit.)
> Avicenna (99 cit.)
> Profatius (91 cit.)
> Robert Grosseteste (84 cit.)
> Gerbert (79 cit.)
> Gerardus Cremonensis (79 cit.)
> Alcabitius (68 cit.)
> Campanus (63 cit.)
> Averroes (62 cit.)
> Johannes de Sacrobosco (56 cit.)
> Roger Bacon (32 cit.)
> Ettore Ausonio (30 cit.)
> Isidore of Seville (21 cit.)
> Petrus de Alliaco (18 cit.)

An analysis of the distribution of the names of scribes and all other cited names could be made by the same procedure. In this manner indexes of names can be created which are also of great interest in other fields of medieval research.

Finally, the ability to link at will the indexed terms and hence names with one another in a search procedure allows one to establish the distribution of the co-citation of names in different manuscripts and historical periods.

OUTLOOK

As is the case with most established smaller databanks, the ICC MSM is not sufficiently well-known. The number of searches conducted lies between 10 and 15 per month. Thus a link-up with national or international computer networks is at present not justified. After a period of two or three years, in which quality and homogeneity of data will be constantly improved, the necessity of a link-up should be reviewed again.

Among the significant results of the work done with the ICC MSM is the discovery of a series of heretofore unknown mathematical texts or other redactions of known texts and the correction of errors in existing manuscript descriptions. Future use of the ICC MSM will provide new impulses not only to research in the history of mathematics but also for interdisciplinary aspects of classical, medieval and renaissance studies. The printing of selected portions of the databank could serve as a basis for new reference works.

And finally, the use of statistical procedures allows scientometric studies to be conducted which can lead to new, qualitatively verifiable insights into mathematical thought in the Middle Ages.

REFERENCES

Eis, G. (1962). *Mittelalterliche Fachliteratur*. Stuttgart: J. B. Metzler. 2 ed. 1967.

Folkerts, M. (1984). Materialien zur Geschichte der europäischen Mathematik in Mittelalter und Renaissance. Ein Projekt der Universitäten Oldenburg und München. In *Jahrbuch der Historischen Forschung in der Bundesrepublik Deutschland. Berichtsjahr 1984* (pp. 36-41). München.

———— (1988). *Mathematische Texte in den westlichen Nationalsprachen im späten Mittelalter*. Lecture held in the Deutsches Museum, Munich, 22 February 1988.

Folkerts, M. and Kühne, A. *The Use of Computers in Cataloging Medieval and Renaissance Manuscripts*. Papers from the International Workshop in Munich, 10-12 August 1989 (1990). In *Algorismus*, Studien zur Geschichte der Mathematik und der Naturwissenschaften, ed. M. Folkerts. München: Institut für Geschichte der Naturwissenschaften.

Geuenich, G. (1988). A data base for research on names and groups of persons in the middle ages. In *Data Base Oriented Source Editions*. *Papers from two sessions at the 23rd International Congress on Medieval Studies, Kalamazoo, Michigan, 5-8 May, 1988* (pp. 9-14).

Gunther, R. W. T. (1938). *Early Science in Oxford* (Vol. 2, pp. 42-43). Oxford University Press, 1921-1945, 14 vols.

Hahn, N. L., Smith, J. B., Stevens, W. M., Sorensson, B. L. (1983). *The Benjamin Data Bank and BAG/2. A case history and user manual for encoding, storing, and retrieving information on Medieval manuscripts*. Winnipeg: Overdale Books.

Klemm, F. (1982). *Dokumentation zur Technikgeschichte des Mittelalters und der Renaissance*. München: Bibliothek des Deutschen Museums.

Kühne, A. (1990). Der Aufbau und die Nutzungsmöglichkeiten einer Datenbank der mathematischen Hand-schriften des Mittelalters und der Renaissance. In *The Use of Computers* (1990), pp. 123-139.

I.R.H.T. (1988). *Liste des auteurs pour section de l'IRHT*. Paris: unpublished.

Richtlinien Handschriftenkatalogisierung. (1985). Bonn-Bad Godesburg: Deutsche Forschungsgemeinschaft. 4th Edition.

Ruh, K. *et alii* (Eds.). (1978). *Die deutsche Literatur des Mittelalters. Verfasserlexikon*. Berlin: de Gruyter.

Sarton, G. (1962). *Introduction to the History of Science*. Vols. 2, 3. Baltimore: William & Wilkins.

Thaller, M. (1989). Datenbanken als Editionsformen? In *Historische Edition und Computer*. Ed. A. Schwob. Graz: Leykam.

Thorndike, L., Kibre, P. (1963). *A Catalogue of Incipits of Medieval Scientific Writings in Latin*. London: The Medieval Academy of America. Revised.

Van Egmond, W. (1986). *ICC MSM – Guide Book and Encoding Plan*. München: Institut für Geschichte der Naturwissenschaften.

Withrow, G. J. (1988). Why did mathematics begin to take off in the sixteenth century? In *Mathematics from Manuscripts to Print*, ed. C. Hay (pp. 264-269). Oxford: Clarendon.

The Hill Monastic Manuscript Library's Computer Assisted Cataloguing Project

Thomas L. Amos

SUMMARY. With over 72,000 manuscripts on microfilm, the Hill Library has developed a computer-assisted cataloguing system for bibliographic control and access to texts in microfilmed manuscripts. We use a microcomputer (IBM PC/XT), data structures, and customized report programs within a proprietary database management system (Ashton-Tate's dBASE III +) to build a database and to publish of catalogues of individual collections. This paper will describe the cataloguing project in light of: (1) selecting the microcomputer hardware and software; (2) use of a relational database as opposed to the various flat-file systems; and (3) the benefits of the computer for bibliographical control.

Eventually, the database will be made available to outside researchers in an on-line format, enhanced by collaboration with other computerized cataloguing projects.

Since the creation of written records and literature and the subsequent development of archives and libraries, librarians have sought adequate means of classifying and providing access to texts contained in a variety of media. Many of the modern library's ideas of how to catalogue books derive from innovations made in medieval libraries. Medieval shelfmarks set a trend that would eventuate into call numbers, and medieval book lists, organized often by author and title, passed through a series of transformations on their way to

Professor Thomas L. Amos is Lecturer in History at Saint John's University and Rare Book Librarian in the Alcuin Library. He is the author of several volumes of a new catalogue of manuscripts of the Fundo Alcobaça, Biblioteca Nacional, Lisbon, and has published several studies of Carolingian sermons.

becoming card catalogue files and on-line cataloguing systems. Gutenberg's revolution and the standardization of forms which it created have, in many ways, separated the needs and methods of cataloguing modern printed books from the strategies employed in cataloguing the surviving medieval manuscripts. Yet manuscript cataloguers deal with many of the same problems and are also engaged in the attempt to apply computer technology to the cataloguing process. Like their printed book counterparts, manuscript cataloguers seek to provide access to a user audience to the often unique resources contained in manuscripts.

In describing the Hill Monastic Manuscript Library's computer cataloguing system,[1] I shall briefly set out the nature of the Library and its holdings in order to assess their problems for the development of a computer assisted system for bibliographical control and access. Second, the origins of the HMML's computer project will be examined in terms of our decision to employ a microcomputer as the hardware base for the project. Finally, I should like to summarize our accomplishments and our plans for the future. This gathering of information should provide a good idea of what it is feasible and possible to do with a microcomputer-based system for the cataloguing of a large collection of manuscripts.

The Hill Monastic Manuscript Library is a sponsored program of Saint John's Abbey and University in Collegeville, Minnesota. Founded in 1965, it has the dual mission of preserving on microfilm the contents of *codices manuscripti* written before 1600, and making these microfilmed manuscripts accessible to the widest possible audience of researchers in the United States and elsewhere. The Hill Library microfilms complete collections of manuscripts from monastic, private, university, municipal, state and national libraries. Over the past twenty-five years, we have conducted microfilming projects in Austria, Spain, Malta, Ethiopia, West Germany, Portugal, Great Britain and the United States. To date, over 72,000 manuscripts, 120,000 papyrus fragments and some 10,000 archival units have been microfilmed. Typical of the collections from which they come, the manuscripts contain individual texts on every conceivable subject, and are written in all of the major western languages. Latin predominates, of course, but we have also microfilmed numerous manuscripts written in Greek, Hebrew, the European vernaculars and in several Middle Eastern and Oriental languages as well.

The Hill Library is a collection of collections, some of which have been acquired through purchase or exchange, but most of which we have microfilmed ourselves. As the microfilming projects continue, the holdings grow at a rate of between 1,200 to 2,000 microfilmed manuscripts annually. The size, diversity and rate of growth of the holdings present major challenges to standard library conceptions of bibliographical control.

The question of bibliographical control is one not easily addressed by a collection as large and diverse as ours. While our current system provides generally adequate control, it can still leave many gaps. We begin with an Inventory Card, containing our Project number for each of the microfilmed manuscripts, the identification of the library holding the original, and the title, date, number of folia or pages and contents of each manuscript. Where possible, these cards are prepared in advance of the filming using printed catalogues. When time is not available or no printed catalogues exist, they are prepared on the filming site using whatever local inventories or *fichiers bibliographiques* that the library possesses. In addition to the Inventory Cards, copies of which are filmed at the head of each microfilmed manuscript, we also microfilm any existing handwritten or typewritten catalogues or inventories, and we acquire copies of all printed catalogues. The quality of these materials varies greatly depending on when and by whom they were done. As a result, our information regarding the manuscripts and the works contained therein ranges from excellent to educated guesses.

The need to make the contents of these sources on microfilm accessible to researchers led the Hill Library to undertake a number of cataloguing projects, and to begin thinking about using computers to aid in the question of bibliographical control. The cataloguing projects, which took a number of forms in the 1960s and 1970s, eventuated in the publication of the *Descriptive Inventories of Manuscripts Microfilmed for the Hill Monastic Manuscript Library, Austrian Libraries* in 1980. This volume was the first of three in a series which have appeared thus far (Yates, 1981; Jeffrey and Yates, 1985; Mayo, 1985). Leaving to one side the larger question of cataloguing from microfilms, the three volumes of this series provided minimal codicological information and reasonably full content descriptions for seven small Austrian collections and for the libraries of St. Georgenberg/Fiecht and Herzogenburg. Each of these volumes admirably serves its intended purpose of providing access to the microfilmed manuscripts and the works they contain. The three- to four-year periods required to produce each catalogue, however, when combined with the ongoing annual growth of the collection demonstrated that using the *Descriptive Inventories* to improve overall bibliographical control simply did not work quickly enough.

Therefore in 1983 a plan was devised for the computerization of the Library's bibliographical records, beginning with the Inventory Cards. This plan included later stages in which, working from the materials contained on the cards, cataloguers would add additional information from the microfilms. A full account of contents and codicological information would eventually be compiled for each microfilmed manuscript. It was at that point that all parties involved began to realize some fundamental things about the nature of computers and the needs of a microfilm manuscript library. No matter how efficient the computer, data still needs to be entered before it can be manipulated and retrieved. The outsiders helped us to realize that two bottlenecks would always be present: acquiring a large body of new catalogue information and entering that information into the computer would both require a great deal of time. By the end of 1984, the project had collapsed of its own weight.

The time had clearly passed for the establishment of any catalogue-based degree of retrospective bibliographical control. Rethinking the situation, it was decided to develop a computer system that would aid in the publication of the Descriptive Inventories and, at the same time, serve as the basis for what would eventually become a database of catalogue description materials. This is where things stood at the time of my own involvement with the Hill Library's computerization project.

The conceptual model — a database that would both hold materials for the current cataloguing project and preserve them permanently as an independent computer-based file — seemed workable. Such a conceptual model for our use of the computer, however, meant abandoning immediate, i.e., five to seven year, computerized bibliographical control. Instead, we would be building a database of manuscript descriptions incrementally through our various cataloguing projects. If the software employed was sufficiently flexible, the resulting system would also permit us retrospectively to enter data for previously catalogued collections. The problems remaining involved selecting a software and hardware platform.

At that time, there were not many manuscript or microfilm libraries that employed computer database systems. Those systems which did exist in any sort of finished form—The Benjamin Data Bank, the FAMULUS program, and the PCC-Project at Nijmegen (Hahn, et alii 1983; McCrank and Bally, 1978; Beinama and Geurts, 1987)[2]—were programs written for mainframe computers. From our own particular point of view, such programs seemed to offer more negative features than benefits. Our costs for mainframe access and storage would be extremely high. When it came to selecting new hardware and upgrading system software, such choices would be made by people who would not have to consult or inform us in the process. We would be totally dependent on outside support for the necessary programming to create, modify and maintain any sort of cataloguing program. Academic mainframes of the type to which we would have access also have periods of use in which access is limited by administrative or academic demands, and there is always a percentage of time when the entire system is "down" for routine or unexpected maintenance. Although mainframes offered large storage capacity and processing power, they did not seem to fit into our institutional pattern.

We sought, therefore, an affordable computer system which would give us a powerful and flexible software environment, sufficient processing and storage capability to handle a reasonable percentage of the collection and which would be reasonably easy to learn. This last criterion was significant. The cataloguing staff at the Hill Library is composed of people whose primary field is some area of medieval studies who are at the Library on a temporary basis, and there tends to be a fairly rapid turnover.

It was already apparent in 1985 that the Intel 8088 and the new 80286 processors had established industry standards around the IBM PC-XT and AT model computers and the DOS operating system. The internal architecture of the microprocessors would permit upward compatibility, so that application software and program files which ran on one machine within this "family" of processors would be able to run on the next higher version. Existing computers by a variety of manufacturers offered respectable processing speed and storage capacity. At that time, the claim was being made that within ten years microcomputers would have the processing and storage capabilities of small mainframes. With the appearance of the Intel 80386 chip and the 600 MB Winchester hard disk drive, it took less than five years to fulfill that prediction. Therefore we decided that it would be possible to begin our system with a software platform that would operate on any of the IBM-compatible machines. When the amount of data in the system required a larger and more powerful machine, it would be relatively easy to upgrade hardware and software as necessary. After the transfer of data to a new machine, the older unit could be put to other uses or become part of a network of linked machines. Although we did begin from the selection of software, as recommended by computer experts, what we knew about existing and future capabilities of our desired hardware platform greatly influenced our decision.

The software platform selected was the proprietary relational database management system dBASE III + by Ashton-Tate. Our software requirements were power, flexibility and relative ease of learning. These could best be obtained from a relational database, which would allow us to establish separate files for codicological information and contents entries for each manuscript. The program would then allow us to relate these files in a variety of ways for searches, queries and reports. With dBASE III + it was also clear that we would be dealing with a well-established commercial software program that would give us as much of a guarantee of future growth and upgrades as the computer industry permits. The program has a strong basic engine which permits the creation of large databases containing multiple related files which have complex field structures. The optional user-interface shell, the Assistant, is menu-driven and gives the novice user quick access to most of the program's resources. Behind the shell lie the command structures accessed from the dot prompt and the dBASE programming language. The dBASE language is similar in form and syntax to Pascal, and it permits the creation of customized reports, user-designed menu and query structures and a variety of other specialized features which do not already exist within the program. Since dBASE III + has such a large user audience, there are also many third-party add-on programs available, such as compilers which increase the efficiency of dBASE language programs.

The main files in our cataloguing system store and retrieve codicological and contents data — field lists and screen data-entry structures for these two files can be found as an appendix. As the system developed, we added to it files for end-leaf materials, additional incipits for sermon and letter collections and an iconographic file for descriptions of initials and illuminations. One additional file, called Runover, allows descriptive information which is too lengthy to fit into fields in other files to "run over" into a linked file. The additional information can be called up from the Runover file by the report program or written to the screen for editing or consultation.

As is the case with all other manuscript cataloguing projects, our system is an independent development. Most manuscript catalogues — and their electronic counterparts — supply the researcher with roughly the same kinds of information. One usually finds a section on codicology — the science of the book or *codex* — which provides information on the physical layout of the manuscript: number of folia; arrangement of quires; framing and ruling scheme; script and number of hands and so on. Content sections will give such information as author and title (where they exist), manuscript *titulus*, incipit (opening words of the text), explicit (last words of the text), colophon, other manuscripts and editions, if any, of the text. There are, with two exceptions,[3] no standard formats for organizing this material, and some catalogues, whether printed and computer-based, offer more information than others. Currently, there is no momentum behind the creation of a single standard format. The AACR rules (second edition) and the MARC formats derived from them do not at the moment provide much help in this area. Based as they are on the idea of standard forms resulting from the uniformity of printed books, they offer too many difficulties for a world in which each manuscript and each copy of a given text are unique and require special descriptions of their own. Our own system of files within dBASE III + allows us to provide a good level of descriptive information for the microfilmed manuscripts and the works which they contain.

The nature of a relational database makes it easy to tie information from the various files together for a single manuscript or a range of manuscripts to manipulate the data or create reports. At present, this system runs on a hardware platform consisting of an IBM PC XT with a twenty megabyte hard disk drive and an IOMEGA twenty megabyte Bernoulli Box for storage and backup. At this point in the development of our system a larger hard disk drive would have been more of a luxury than a necessity. The Bernoulli cartridge system permits segmented storage of large amounts of data on its individual ten megabyte cartridges.

Our computer project began with the Hill Library's current cataloguing project, preparation of a three-volume catalogue of the 456 manuscripts of the *Fundo Alcobaça* of the Biblioteca Nacional, Lisbon. This collection has been little-known to scholarship outside of Portugal, and the significance of the manuscripts seemed to make it a good choice for initiating the computer system. Data entry of the cataloguing materials was done at the keyboard using the data entry screens which we had designed for dBASE III + . What remained was to produce useful and usable output.

The key feature of our current system is a report program, written in the dBASE language, which draws materials from these files together for the production of our catalogue volumes. A major weakness of all commercial database management systems for the storage of text materials is the fact that they generally produce reports as tables based on columns of numbers or short text strings. Our report program, written with outside help, involves a series of nested modules or subroutines which relate all files for individual manuscripts, and take the data stored from them to arrange it into a codicological paragraph and content entries. Other modules of the program use materials from the related files to produce the main structures for indices of incipits, scribes, dated manuscripts, secundo folio references and a general or author-title-subject index. The main text body and the indices are reported out of this program as ASCII text, which is then entered into a word processing program for the addition of diacritical marks and final formatting. For volume I of the Alcobaça catalogue as an example, our report program took about two hours to produce ASCII-text files of approximately 448 kilobytes for the main text and indices. The formatted version of these documents is then printed on a laser printer to produce camera-ready copy for the catalogue volume.

To date, this system has helped to produce two volumes of a catalogue for the manuscripts of the *Fundo Alcobaça* of the Biblioteca Nacional of Portugal and a third volume is in preparation (Amos, 1989; Amos and Black, 1990). Our database currently stands at around 500 manuscript descriptions which include 456 microfilmed manuscripts from the *Fundo Alcobaça*, ten actual manuscripts owned by the Library and some fifty other miscellaneous items. Since I have devoted much of this paper to describing how our computer system supports the Library's cataloguing activities, let me conclude with a brief account of our plans for the database as an independent entity.

Immediate plans involve an upgrading of the hardware platform. Permitting outside access to the database will require a faster, more powerful machine than our current PC/XT to support a menu driven query structure accessible via modem. We plan in the next two years to upgrade to the Intel 80386 processing chip in a computer with a much larger hard disk drive. A more powerful machine will also improve the efficiency of the report program—the document which required two hours to produce on the PC/XT will require around forty-five minutes on the Intel 80386. Acquisition of additional computers will permit cataloguers to enter data directly into the system from their own work areas. These additional computers may well be connected together by a Local Area Network (LAN) to permit more efficient sharing of files and peripheral resources. While the software base will probably be upgraded to dBASE IV, we shall wait for a version without the current "bugs" and with better implementation of the Structured Query Language (SQL) conventions.

Over the next three years, we plan to add another 700 manuscript descriptions to our database. Approximately 400 of these will come from the next cataloguing project, and the remainder represent existing catalogue descriptions which will be entered into the system. With around 1,200 descriptions from ten collections in the database at that point, there should be sufficient material to attract interest in it. It would be wasteful to devote time prematurely to a service to which no one wishes to avail oneself. But after this critical mass of information has been achieved, we plan to make it available for outside researchers to consult through a modem.

In preparation for that type of access, we are currently planning out a menu-based read-only query shell in the dBASE language. The shell will permit the asking of questions derived from a menu, and will prevent unlimited and uncontrolled access to the data in the files. Programs already existing which will be subroutines of the menu-driven query shell are a search program which converts variants of spelling and usage in the incipits to standard forms and a concordance program which permits searching incipits by keywords. The planned menu-driven query system will offer the outside researcher an opportunity to use available computerized cataloguing materials at a distance, and will offer us reasonable security for our files. As part of this system, we are also beginning to explore ways to make our card catalogue of over a million Latin and western vernacular incipits available on the computer. This particular element of our plans is very long-range in terms of the time it will require to make such data accessible, but it is an option which we will continue to investigate.

On the whole our experience with the microcomputer has been favorable in terms of the balance between the cost in time and resources necessary to create the system and the returns in efficiency we receive from it. The computer cataloguing system has allowed us to improve substantially the format of the *Descriptive Inventory* series. We have only begun to employ the new methods and options of working with the cataloguing data that it provides. One lesson that we have learned concerning software is that a relational database system provides much more flexibility than a flat-file system. As a corollary, I would add that no software package whatsoever should be used for a project of this nature unless it also offers an internal programming language. A strong programming language permits modifications and report programs to be grafted on to the main storage and retrieval system. Unless a storage and retrieval system is perfect from the outset, the need for such additions will inevitably appear.

As for the choice between mainframes and microcomputers, Ecclesiastes noted long ago that "the race was not always to the swift, nor the battle to the strong." It is perfectly feasible to begin a manuscript or microfilm manuscript cataloguing project on a microcomputer. The great range of processing chips and high-density storage devices currently available makes that observation even more true now than when we began the Hill Library project four years ago. The relatively easy ability to upgrade allows one to begin a project with one machine and to finish it on a larger machine or a local area network of connected machines. The experience of the Hill Library with microcomputers is not exhaustive, certainly, but it does demonstrate the fact that microcomputers have an independent role in computerized manuscript cataloguing projects.

NOTES

1. An earlier version of this paper was presented at the XVIIIth International Congress on History of Science, Hamburg/Munich, August 1-9, 1989. I would like to thank S. Eva Hooker, C.S.C., Academic Vice-President of Saint John's University, and especially Rev. Hilary Thimmesh, O.S.B., President of Saint John's University, for travel support which made presentation of the paper possible, along with Dr. Julian Plante, Executive Director of the Hill Library. My colleague at the Hill Library, Dr. Jonathan Black, made several suggestions from which this version has benefitted.

2. The FAMULUS program created by McCrank and Batty for the Mt. Angel catalogue was not applied to it. I would like to thank Professor Wesley Stevens for supplying me with a copy of the work by Beinama and Geurts (1987).

3. The exceptions for standard formats apply to manuscript cataloguing projects in West Germany which are guided by the *Richtlinien* (1985) and the recent series of catalogues produced in Austria which are governed by the rules set out by Otto Mazal (1975). One other proposed set of standards can be found in Beaud-Gambier and Fossier (1977).

REFERENCES

Amos, T. L. (1990). A First-level approach to sharing information from manuscript description databases. In *The Use of Computers* (1990), pp. 1-18.

———— (1989). *The Manuscripts of the Fundo Alcobaça of the Biblioteca Nacional, Lisbon*, Vol. 1: Manuscripts 1-150, Descriptive Inventories . . . ; Vol. 2: Manuscripts 151-301. Portuguese Libraries. Collegeville, Minnesota: Hill Monastic Manuscript Library, Saint John's University.

Amos, T. L., Black, J. G. *The Manuscripts of the Fundo Alcobaça of the Biblioteca Nacional*, Vol. 3 (in press).

Beaud-Gambier, M.-J., Fossier, L. (1977). *Guide pour l'elaboration d'une notice de manuscrit*. Paris: Institut de Recherche et d'Histoire des Textes.

Beinema, P. F., Geurts, A. J. (1987). Computer supported codicography of medieval manuscripts. An evaluation of the PCC-Project. In *Ontsluiting van Middeleeuwse Handschriften in de Nederlanden*, ed. A. J. Geurts (pp. 223-235). Nijmegen/Grave.

Hahn, N. L., Smith, J. B., Stevens, W. M., Sorenson, L. B. (1983). *The Benjamin Data Bank and BAG/2: A case history and user manual for encoding, storing, and retrieving information on Medieval manuscripts*. Winnipeg, Manitoba.

Jeffrey, P., Yates, D. (1985). *St. Georgenburg-Fiecht*. Austrian libraries: Vol. 2. Collegeville, Minnesota: Hill Monastic Manuscript Library, Saint John's University.

Mayo, H. (1985). *Herzogenburg*. Austrian libraries: Vol. 3. Collegeville, Minnesota: Hill Monastic Manuscript Library.

Mazal, O. (Ed.). (1975). *Handschriftenbeschreibung in Österreich*. Österreichische Akademie der Wissenschaften, Philosophisch-Historische Klasse, Denkschriften, 122. Vienna.

McCrank, L. J., Batty, C. D. (1978). The Mt. Angel Abbey manuscript and rare books project: Cataloguing with FAMULUS. *Computers and the Humanities 12*, 215-222.

Richtlinien Handschriftenkatalogisierung (1985). 4th ed. Bonn-Bad Godesburg: Deutsche Forschungsgemeinschaft.

Yates, Donald. (1981). *Geras, Güssing, Haus, Innsbruck Wilten, Salzburg E.b. Konsistorialarchiv, Salzburg E.b. Priesterseminar, Salzburg Museum Carolino-Augusteum*. Austrian libraries: Vol. 1. Collegeville, Minnesota: Hill Monastic Manuscript Library, Saint John's University.

The Corpus of Greek
Medical Manuscripts:
A Computerized Inventory
and Catalogue

Alain Touwaide

SUMMARY. The *Corpus of Greek Medical Manuscripts* is a new research programme which intends to supersede the old repertory of Herman Diels. Its purpose is to inventory anew the medical manuscripts, to describe them fully from the originals, to treat the detailed information by help of the computer, and to establish a microfilm collection of the manuscripts. It will constitute a first-hand materials for a history of medicine based on the factual data contained in the manuscripts.

1. INTRODUCTION

In the field of Greek medieval books, the medical manuscript has a special status: it was useful. Its contents, the medical texts, made it practical and indeed immediately more useable than most other books. This was its special characteristic.

As a result, the medical *codex manuscriptus* often bears traces of its use: ex libris, notes of owners, practical annotations, results of therapies, and other unique entries — all things of great interest for the historian of science. Through a systematic study of these elements, the historian can indeed reach a factual level in history of medicine that is realistic and experiential. In doing so, he will write a history which is complementary to that other history which is more like a superstructure. Ordinary history is usually drawn from documents, schools, ideas and their evolution; although that is in-

---

Dr. Alain Touwaide has published the Greek text with French translation of the two toxicological treatises ascribed to Dioscorides, and other studies on medical literature of ancient Greece and Byzatium.

75

teresting and even indispensable, it is often a history which has not reached the men themselves, the healers or patients, their illnesses or experiences. One needs the kind of history that is based on details, the details which are between the lines of a text, remarks which are left in margins by a physician, the many things that may be found in the manuscript pages.

It must be recognized however that until recently Greek medical manuscripts have not been studied in such a way as to reveal all the information they contain to make this factual history of medicine. Unfortunately most of the manuscripts themselves have been largely neglected and their contents unknown because they have not been specifically and systematically catalogued and analyzed.

2. *STATUS QUAESTIONIS*

Several efforts to describe medical texts and their codices were undertaken by the C. Daremberg (France), G. A. Costomiris (Greece), and other scholars during the nineteenth century.[1] Many Greek, Arabic, and Latin medical manuscripts were catalogued at the beginning of the twentieth century by German philologists under the direction of Hermann Diels (1906-1907).[2] The result was an inventory of manuscripts according to authors and their treatises, so far as known at that time. Thus for each author and treatise, the repertoried manuscripts are presented in alphabetical order of the name of cities in which they were conserved, with a brief mention of their century of when copied and the pages on which the texts were transcribed.

This work is of great interest and still useful, even if it suffers of a number of faults, due to the epoch in which it was prepared and to the conception of the project itself. An insufficient knowledge of ancient and Byzantine medicine may be attributed to the epoch, with the consequent ignorance or reject of medical authors who are known or at least better appreciated today. Inadequacies in the inventory and cataloguing of manuscripts can also be attributed to the epoch, since *codices* then escaped notice altogether which reveal themselves today to be very important.

On the other hand the deliberately chosen method of excessively brief description of the inventoried manuscripts will be attributed to the project itself: shelfmark, century of transcription, and pages of text; incorrect shelfmarks and confusion between Greek and Latin manuscripts; description of the same manuscript at various locations without notice of subsequent change of owners. Some of these problems of course derived from the use of old printed catalogues which gave incomplete data, instead of direct and personal examination of manuscripts.

Since the publication of the work, some of the manuscripts or entire collections have been sold or destroyed (especially during World War II) so that the actual situation of manuscripts' conservation may no longer correspond with the one known to Diels and his staff.

For all these reasons, Diels is only a starting-point for the inventory of the manuscripts of a Greek medical treatise; and it certainly does not exempt the research scholar from a personal and direct consultation of manuscripts' catalogues to identify all the surviving *codices* which contain a work.[3]

To inventory the Greek manuscripts of medical treatises, the prefaces of the ever increasing number of editions of texts are also available. However these prefaces do not study the manuscripts exhaustively from a codicological point of view; they usually limit themselves to the elements which are necessary for an edition of the text itself, even if in some cases they use codicology and paleography. Such a way of working is normal, due to the fact that the study of manuscripts is only an aid for an edition and not an end in itself. Even if these editions offer some elements relevant to the needs of cataloguing — and fortunately they often do so, they do not do so systematically, being produced without a general plan of publication throughout the world. As a consequence of these limited resources, large parts of ancient Greek medicine have yet to be discovered.

3. CORPUS OF GREEK MEDICAL MANUSCRIPTS

General definition. Given this situation and with the purpose of furnishing better information to historians of ancient Greek medicine about texts and additional historical entries which reveal the use of texts which are contained in manuscripts, a *Corpus of Greek Medical Manuscripts* was proposed in 1986 with a triple objective:

3.1 To inventory all the known manuscripts of the various Greek medical treatises (with or without the name of the author) on the model of Diels' catalogue; the new *Corpus* will not be limited to classical and Byzantine medicine but will include also modern Greek medical science.

3.2 To describe these manuscripts from inspection of the original *codices* themselves with the most effective current methods of codicology, and especially to take notice of all the elements relevant to a factual history of medicine.

3.3 To copy all of these manuscripts on microfilm and constitute a microfilm collection and to place them at the disposition of interested scholars. For this purpose it was also decided to use the computer to create the necessary database in order that the information could be often revised, updated and easily retrieved for research.

4. PREPARATION OF THE CORPUS, FIRST PHASE

Inventory of manuscripts. Before collecting the information relevant to the program of the *Corpus*, it has been necessary to constitute *instrumenta* adapted to the purpose of the programme:

4.1 An index of the manuscripts quoted in the Diels has been established which classifies the items by country, city, library, and series. In doing this work, the exactitude of the information furnished by the Diels has been verified by the consultation of libraries' printed catalogues used by Diels' staff and mentioned in the bibliography of the work. This index has revealed a total of about 1,800 manuscripts dispersed throughout the whole of Europe, but only Europe. The result of this classification is a card-index, with the mention of the manuscripts and the references of their citations in the Diels, whether or not they are correct.

4.2 In a second step, the actual validity of the information furnished by Diels has been established by verifying the actual presence of the manuscripts in the libraries in which they were during 1906-1907, and the shelf-mark of each one. This work has been realized by a double control: verifica-

tion in modern printed catalogues and direct enquiry to con-
servators of the libraries. When necessary, the information
has been up-dated with indication of the new location,
shelf-mark, and every other element, or with mention that
the manuscript has been destroyed.

4.3 Finally, the manuscripts have been inventoried once again
ab nihilo on the basis of the available modern printed library
catalogues inventoried by the so-called Richard (1958, with
additions in 1964) and with current bibliography.[4]

This inventory has permitted us to catalogue about 2,200 manuscripts, i.e., 22% more than in the Diels, including also modern
Greek manuscripts. A card index has been created with the location
of the manuscripts, their shelf-marks, and bibliographic references
to catalogues, books, articles or studies mentioning them. Furthermore the pages of catalogues in which the inventoried manuscripts
are described have been copied (xerox-copies) and registered in alphabetical order of location (i.e., country, city, library successively), to create a local reference library of information about
Greek medical texts and manuscripts.

5. PREPARATION OF THE CORPUS, SECOND PHASE

Inventory of authors and treatises. Simultaneously an inquiry has
been made in the field of the history of Greek ancient, medieval and
even modern medicine to establish an inventory of authors, works,
and editions. This has led to the constitution of the following working materials:

5.1 Index-cards of Greek authors and treatises, with biographic
material from the *Realencyklopädie*, the *Dictionary of Scientific Biography*, or other relevant bibliographic material.[5]

5.2 Index-cards of the most recent critical edition of each treatise, studies of manuscript tradition, and history of the text.

5.3 Acquisition or copy of bibliographical material (sub 5.2) in
order to constitute a library specialized in the field of Greek
medical texts.

6. PREPARATION OF THE CORPUS: THIRD PHASE

Codicological bibliography and book collection. In order to create an efficient codicological method to analyse the manuscripts — since there is no one at disposition (de quo vide infra, sub 7) — the codicological field has been studied and a bibliography of the published material has been constituted. It consists in an analytic card-index based upon the current bibliography as known through the specialised journals, e.g., *Scriptorium, Byzantinische Zeitschrift, L'Année philologique*, and *Bulletin signalétique*. The most important materials have been acquired or copied (xerox-copies), constituting a reference collection in the field of codicology.

7. PREPARATION OF THE CORPUS: FOURTH PHASE

Codicological method for manuscripts description. After collecting all these materials, the following phase in the preparation of the *Corpus* was to constitute a method for manuscripts description with a double aim:

7.1 To permit recognition of all elements of the manuscripts which could contribute to the construction of a factual history of ancient medicine, as described in the introduction (vide sub 1).

7.2 To permit computerized exploitation of these elements, i.e., the constitution of indices of all aspects of the codices in order to group manuscripts on the base of their various aspects.

The various methods available — the *Leges* of the Biblioteca Apostolica Vaticana (Devresse, 1954, pp. 282-285), the *Richtlinien* (1985) of the Deutsche Forschungsgemeinschaft, the *Guide* (1977) of the Institut Recherche et d'Histoire des Textes, the method of Nijmegen University (Geurts, Gruijs, Van Krieken, 1983), or the norms of the Italian standard catalogue (Jemolo, Morelli, 1984) for example — have been studied and compared. This study led to development of a method particularly adapted for this case, viz. collecting all the significative elements of the comprehensive history of the *codices*, from the act of copying even to its practical use by a physician.

This method has been submitted in printed form to the greatest experts in the field throughout the world (de quo vide infra, sub 12.2) and has received their approval. The forms are reproduced at the conclusion of this essay.

8. PREPARATION OF THE CORPUS, FIFTH PHASE

Computerization. The fifth phase in the preparation of the *Corpus* consisted in the adaptation of the codicological method described here above (sub 7) to the computer. It has been decided to implant this application on a configuration PC, type IBM/compatible, with hard-disk and with a memory unit of 40 MB in order to promote the largest compatibility and moreover the greatest flexibility. For this purpose a programme was written in dBase III[6] which follows exactly the form elaborated for the manuscript description as described above.

The result is a multi-screen program with a certain number of items corresponding to the items of the form. Each one of these items has an abbreviated name, indicating the aspect of the manuscript which is concerned, and a field of variable length for encoding of data of the manuscripts. This encoding may take the form of Binary choice: Y[es] or N[o];

> Numeric datum; or
> Alphabetic datum.

The way in which the data must be registered has been fixed in a *User's guide* available to collaborators of the programme (de quo vide infra, sub 12.3). The enregistered data are permanently indexed in order to create a permanently up-dated data-base. Theoretically indices could be produced for all the items of the manuscript descriptions. But in practice only the following indices are produced because of their interest and utility, not only for the *Corpus* but also generally speaking for codicological research:

8.2.1 Index of manuscripts classified in alphabetical order (names of country, city, and library successively) in the original spelling of the names; within this field classification is in numeric order of shelf-mark.

8.2.2 Index of watermarks collected in the manuscripts analysed, with the identification in the commonly used repertories between brackets (Briquet, 1968; Likhacev, 1899; Mosin, Trajlic, 1957; *Monumenta*, 1950 seq.; Harlfinger, 1974, 1980). Each item is followed by citation of the manuscript in which it appears, with indication of the pages.

8.2.3 Index of centuries, period or years, or date of each manuscript copy and, within this chronological classification, an index of places of copying. Each item is followed by citation of manuscripts copied in each century, period of years, or date and in place.

8.2.4 Index of places of copying, and an index of centuries, period of years, or date of copying within that geographical classification; each item is followed by citation of manuscripts copied in each place and in each time.

8.2.5 Index of copists with citation of manuscripts and pages produced.

8.2.6 Index of owners (private) indicating their dates of birth and death; each name is followed by the indication of the manuscripts owned.

8.2.7 Index of authors and texts with citation of manuscripts and pages in which the designated texts appear. At the fulfillment of the research-program, this classification will replace Diels' catalogue.

9. PREPARATION OF THE CORPUS, SIXTH PHASE

Experimentation. In order to verify the validity of all these preliminary phases, the method has been tested in four ways:

9.1 Inventory of the medical manuscripts of the following libraries according to the printed catalogues available:

9.1.1. El Escorial (Spain), Biblioteca del Real Monasterio (Revilla, 1936; De Andres, 1965, 1967, 1968).

9.1.2. Leiden (The Netherlands), Rijksuniversiteitsbibliotheek (Molhuysen 1910; De Meyier, 1946, 1955).
9.1.3. Milano (Italy), Biblioteca Ambrosiana (Martini,
Bassi 1906).
9.1.4. Vaticano (Città del), Biblioteca Apostolica Vaticana:
Vaticani graeci, Barberiniani graeci, Borgianai
graeci, Chisiani graeci, Ottoboniani graeci, Palatini
graeci, Reginenses graeci, Pii II graeci, Rossiani
graeci, Urbinates graeci, Archivio di S. Pietro).[7]

For each library all the repertoried manuscripts have been registered and indexed in a card-index, and the various indexes here
described (vide supra, sub 8.2.1. to 8.2.7.) have been produced.
The interest of the indices has been established by the grouping of
manuscripts which had never been done before.

9.2 Description of the manuscripts of the Biblioteca Ambrosiana in Milano from first-hand inspection with the help of
the description method presented above. About fifty manuscripts were used in a trial to test the efficiency of the
method and the feasibility of collecting data directly from
manuscripts, rather than from other sources. It has been
found that the analysis of an entire manuscript requires a
mean time of two hours, obviously with a possible variation
due to the importance of the codex. This result has been
judged positive.

On the other hand the method has permitted collection of all the
data contained in the manuscripts without omitting any aspect.
Once again the result was positive and the method appears to be
feasible.

9.3 Inventory of all the extant manuscripts of two completely
different medical works: on the one hand, the *Alexipharmaka* and *Theriaka* of the second century B.C. Alexandrian
Greek poet Nicander; and on the other, the well known first
century A.D. *Materia medica* of Dioscorides. As for Nicander, the result was a list of 31 manuscripts instead of the 18
mentioned in Gow and Scholfield (1953, pp.9-11). As for

Dioscorides no less than about 250 manuscripts were identified instead of the 28 mentioned in the Wellmann edition, v. 2, pp. v-xxv (see also Riddle 1985). Once again, this result has been judged positive, if not spectacular.

9.4. Encoding and indexing of the data collected on all forty of the extant manuscripts of Pseudo-Dioscorides toxicological treatises (Touwaide, 1981), in order to verify both feasibility of encoding and efficiency of the indexing and retrieval programme.

10. CONCLUSION OF THE PREPARATION

Realisation. At the end of the sixth phase of preparation and experimentation, the research program of the *Corpus of Greek Medical Manuscripts* has been estimated both feasible and desirable. In consequence at the end of 1988 it was presented to an international college of experts and received a positive judgment. Therefore the program entered in an operative phase, its realisation, which is still in course.

11. REALISATION OF THE CORPUS

The microfilm collection. Since one of the purposes of the *Corpus* program is to create a micro-film collection of Greek medical manuscripts, the feasibility of this part of the program has also been tested. A copy of each of the 31 inventoried manuscripts of Nicander and the 250 Dioscorides manuscripts has been ordered from the various libraries in which they are conserved. So far about 300 microfilms of those manuscripts have been collected, in addition to 50 microfilms of Pseudo-Dioscorides' toxicological treatises already owned by the author; the total will soon be 350 microfilms.

All the microfilms have been received in rolls which are difficult to conserve and to consult, especially for consulting a single page on a roll. Thus it seemed easier to conserve these microfilms in jackets (148 x 105 mm) of two times six views, i.e., 12 views per jacket or 6 double manuscript pages. These jackets present in the upper margin a white part on which one can write the name of the manuscript, its shelf-mark, and the pages contained within the jacket, making it easy to find a certain page of a consulted manuscript. Jackets of a manuscript were placed in a plastic pocket especially created for this purpose and bearing an adhesive label with the manuscript identification. In this way it seemed possible to constitute a large microfilm collection, easy to conserve and convenient to consult.

Organisation. Given the important number of codices to analyze which number 2.200 according to our estimate (de quo vide supra sub 4.3), it seemed necessary to associate to the program the largest number of collaborators, considering not only the personal interest of various authors and the diverse locations of the manuscripts themselves. On the other hand it appeared desirable to place the *Corpus* under supervision of collaborators with special competencies acquired in the various disciplines involved in the programme, especially in the fields of palaeography, codicology, history of collections and of libraries, in order to ensure the highest scientific level.

Such a way of working rendered absolutely necessary a central unit of organisation and coordination, namely the unit in which all the material relevant to the programme are conserved (i.e., bibliographies, Greek texts, various studies, xerox-copies, card-indexes, data-base, microfilm collection). The result is a three-level network with:

11.1 A central unit which conserves all the material generated by the programme which plans and coordinates the realisation of the *Corpus*, ensures its computerisation and publication, and also ensures the continued development of the database.
11.2 A scientific committee which guarantees the high level of the general enterprise and of each of its realisations and publications.
11.3 A network of collaborators who furnish the description of the manuscripts by use of forms created for this purpose (de quo vide supra sub 7).

Communication of the results. To ensure that scholars may receive the results of this research programme as soon as possible and preferably before the completion of the work, a flexible, two-fold means of communication has been chosen, resulting from the analysis of that used by comparable research programmes such as the *Aristoteles graecus* of Berlin.

On the one hand there will be an annual microfiche publication (148 × 105 mm) of the available manuscript descriptions, with printed indices. In these microfiche each manuscript receives a sequential Arabic project number writ large so that it can be read without placing the microfiche on the reader apparatus. The manuscript descriptions constitute additive information, with new descriptions added each year to previously published ones in sequence. Consequently there will also be added a register of manuscripts which identifies them by location, library, and shelfmark, followed by the indication of their number on the microfiches, so that they can easily be found. Indices however are published on paper, so that they can be consulted simultaneously with the microfiches. Their information is cumulative, i.e., every year a new version is made to include the new material published during the year, so that indexes are perpetually up-dated. Both microfiche and the indices will be published as a volume of about 400 pages every year and will be made available by subscription.

A database on the computer will be available. In a first stage this database might be consulted at the central unit, personally or on request. Later it should become accessible on-line if possible, in a way which must still be defined.

12. ACTUAL STATUS AND EVOLUTION OF THE CORPUS

By the Summer of 1990 the following results have already been reached:

12.1 Inventory of about 2.200 manuscripts on the basis of extant printed catalogues; reference library begun with xerox-copies of catalogue pages on which the manuscripts are described.

12.2 Personal analysis of manuscripts by the author or by collaborators and creation of new descriptions of those in the following collections:

- 50 manuscripts of Biblioteca Ambrosiana, Milano;
- 6 manuscripts of Biblioteca universitaria e regionale, Messina, and Biblioteca universitaria e regionale, Palermo (Sicily).
- 40 manuscripts of Pseudo-Dioscorides' two toxicological treatises in various libraries;
- 50 manuscripts in various libraries.

12.3 Microfilm copies of manuscripts containing the following authors or texts:
- 60 manuscripts of Nicander, *Alexipharmaka*, *Theriaka*; scolia; *Paraphrase* of Eutecnius; notes;
- 250 manuscripts of Dioscorides, *De materia medica*;
- 40 manuscripts of Pseudo-Dioscorides' two toxicological treatises;
- 50 manuscripts of other items.

The following collections will be analyzed and described by the author or by collaborators in a near future:

Leiden (The Netherlands), Rijksuniversiteitsbibliotheek (50 mss);

El Escorial (Spain), Real Biblioteca del Monasterio de San Lorenzo (40 mss); Madrid (Spain), Biblioteca Nacional (15 mss); Modena (Italy), Biblioteca Estense (30 mss).

Finally, scholars have already accepted invitation to analyze and describe the following collections:

London (Great-Britain), British Library;
Napoli (Italy), Biblioteca Nazionale;
Mont-Athos (Greece), monastic libraries;
Berlin (Germany), Deutsche Staatsbibliothek.

13. REALISATION OF THE CORPUS

Financial support. From the beginning the *Corpus* has been entirely supported by the author. Obviously the development now planned requires the help of every kind of institution: public, private, academic.

NOTES

1. Only the first part of Daremberg's survey of manuscripts containing Greek medical texts was published (Daremberg, 1853: England incomplete), but there were summaries for his work in Germany (1845) and in England (1848). The unpublished material of Daremberg is conserved in manuscript form in the Académie de médecine (Paris, France), for which an inventory and a brief description was prepared by Boinet (1908, pp. 57-78, nos. 402-542).

Before Daremberg the German physician F. R. Dietz had already begun such a program between 1827 and 1833 with a tour in Europe, but he did not complete his work (Hagen, 1974, p.133). See also Costomiris (1889 seq.).

2. On the history of this project see Kollesch (1973). The catalogue (Diels, 1905, 1906 and 1907) provoked many corrections and additions thereafter, for example Mercati (1938) and the more recent works of Durling (1976, 1982).

Other projects have focused upon limited parts of the history of ancient medicine, for example Thomson (1933), Beaujouan (1962), Kibre (1975 *seq.*). For other periods of the history of medicine, some attempts have also been realised, such as Del Pilar Hitos Natera (1968-1970) and Blanco-Juste (1934-1935). But it must be noted that none have included the full and detailed data from manuscripts, as outlined here. The microfilming program of the National Library of Medicine of the U.S.A. should also be noted; for a brief description see The National Library of Medicine. *A Summary Checklist*.

3. For such a use of the Diels catalogue see, for example, the most recent edition of Hippocratus, *De l'ancienne médecine*, edited by J. Jouanna (1990) who added three manuscripts to the list and omitted another, p.86,n.1.

4. See the bibliography furnished by *Scriptorium*: Bulletin codicologique, *Byzantinische Zeitschrift*, and *Bulletin signalétique*. Also available is a "Liste de catalogues . . . " prepared by the Institut de recherche et d'histoire des textes (Paris, 1986), privately distributed.

5. The bibliography of Greek (ancient and modern) or Byzantine medical authors is enormous. See *Byzantinische Zeitschrift* or *Current Work in the History of Medicine*, an International Bibliography, published by the Wellcome Institute for the History of Medicine, London.

6. This computer program has been conceived and written by D. Touwaide (Brussels).

7. For the *Vaticani graeci*, see Mercati and De'Cavalieri (1923), Devreesse (1937, 1950), Giannelli (1950, 1961), Canart (1970), Lilla (1985). For the *Barberiniani graeci*, see Capocci (1958); the second part has been prepared by the late J. Mogenet and is in print, but in the meantime the inventory of Seymour De Ricci (1907) is still useful. For the *Borgiani* and *Chisiani graeci* see De'Cavalieri (1927); for *Ottoboniani graeci* see Feron and Bataglini (1893); for *Palatini graeci* see Stevenson (1885); for *Reginenses et Pii II greci* see Stevenson (1888); for *Rossiani graeci* see Gollob (1908); and for *Urbinates graeci* see Stornajolo (1895). Manuscripts of the Archivio di S. Pietro now conserved in the Biblioteca Apostolica Vaticana (Canart, 1966).

REFERENCES

Beaujouan, G. (1962). Manuscrits scientifiques médiévaux de l'Université de Salamanque et de ses "Colegios mayores." *Bibliothèque de l'Ecole des Hautes Etudes Hispaniques, 32.* Bordeaux: Féret.

Boinet, A. (1908). *Catalogue des manuscrits de la bibliothèque de l'Académie de médecine.* Paris.

Blanco-Juste, F. M. (1934-1935). Un tesoro de la Biblioteca Escurialense: Manuscritos Arabes, Hispano-Arabes, Turcos, Israelitas y Persas, de asuntos Médicos-Farmacéuticos, que se conservan en tan famosa biblioteca. *El Monitor de la Farmacia y de la Terapéutica, 40,* 473-480; *41,* 1-5, 53-62. Madrid.

Briquet, C. M. (1907). *Les filigranes. Dictionaire historique des margues du papier,* 4 vols. Paris: Picard.

Canart, P. (1970). *Bybliothecae Apostolicae Vaticanae codices manu scripti recensiti Vaticani graeci* (1745-1962). Roma.

———— (1966). Catalogue des manuscrits grecs de l'Archivio di San Pietro. *Studi e Testi. 246.* Roma.

Capocci, V. (1958). *Bybliothecae Apostolicae Vaticanae codices manu scripti recensiti . . . codices Barberiniani graeci,* t. 1 (1-163). Roma.

Costomiris, G. A. (1889-1892, 1897). Etudes sur les écrits inédits des anciens médecins grecs et ceux dont le texte original est perdu, mais existent en latin ou en arabe. *Revue des études grecques* 2, 343-383; *3,* 145-179; *4,* 97-110; *5,* 61-72; *10,* 405-445. Paris.

Daremberg, C. (1845). *Rapport adressé à M. le Ministre de l'instruction publique par C. Daremberg . . . chargé d'une mission médico-littéraire en Allemagne.* Paris.

———— (1848, 4 novembre). Résumé d'un voyage médico-littéraire en Angleterre. *Gazette médicale de Paris.*

———— (1853). *Notices et extraits des manuscrits médicaux grecs, latins et français des principales bibliothèques de l'Europe,* 1. Manuscrits grecs d'Angleterre. Paris.

De Andres, G. (1965, 1967). *Catalogo de los codices griegos de la Real Biblioteca de El Escorial.* 2 vols. Madrid.

———— (1968). *Catalogo de los codices griegos desaparecidos de la Real Biblioteca de El Escorial.* Madrid.

De'Cavalieri, P. Franchi (1927). *Bybliothecae Apostolicae Vaticanae codices manu scripti recensiti . . . Codices graeci Chisiani et Borgiani.*

De Ricci, Seymour (1907). Liste sommaire des manuscrits grecs de la Bibliotheca Barberiniana. *Revue des Bibliothèques 17,* 81-125. Paris.

Del Pilar Hitos Natera, M. (1968-1970). Indice de los manuscritos existentes en la Biblioteca Nacional de Madrid, de interés a la Historia d la Farmacia y Ciencias Afines, con breves comentarios de su contenido. *Boletin de la Sociedad Espanola de Historia de la Farmacia,* 19, 49-72, 117-128, 153-176; *20,* 17-37, 74-82. 103-126, 154-181; *21,* 15-44. 63-91. Madrid.

De Meyier, K. A. (1946, 1955). *Bibliothecae Universitatis Leidensis. Codices manuscripti*, 4. Codices Perizoniani; 6. Codices Vossiani Graeci et Miscellanei. Leiden.

Devreesse, R. (1937). *Bybliothecae Apostolicae Vaticanae codices manu scripti recensiti Vaticani graeci*, t. 2 (330-603). Roma.

―――― (1950). *Bybliothecae Apostolicae Vaticanae codices manu scripti recensiti Vaticani graeci*, t. 3 (604-866). Roma.

―――― (1954). *Introduction à l'étude des manuscrits grecs*. Paris: Impr. nationale, Librairie C. Klincksieck.

Dictionary of Scientific Biography (1970-1980). Ed. C. C. Gillispie et alii. New York: Scribner.

Diels, H. (1905, 1906). Die Handschriften der antiken Ärzte – Griechische Abteilung, I. Hippokrates und Galenos; II. Die übrigen griechischen Ärzte außer Hippokrates und Galenos. *Abhandlungen der Königliche-Preussische Akademie der Wissenschaften, Philos.-historische Klasse*. Berlin.

―――― (1907). Bericht über den Stand des interakademischen Corpus medicorum graecorum und Erster Nachtrag zu den in den Abhandlungen 1905 und 1906 veröffentliche Katalogen: die Handschriften der antiken Ärzte, I und II Teil. *Abhandlungen der Königliche-Preussische Akademie der Wissenschaften, Philos.-historische Klasse*. Berlin.

Durling, R. J. (1976, 1982). Corrigenda and addenda to Diels' Galenica. *Traditio, 13*, 461-476; *37*, 373-381. New York.

Feron, E. and Battaglini F. (1893). *Bybliothecae Apostolicae Vaticanae codices manu scripti recensiti . . . Codices manuscripti graeci Ottoboniani . . .* Roma.

Geurts, A. J., Gruijs, A. and Van Krieken, J. (1983). Codicografie en computer. *Nijmeegse codicologisch Cahiers, 1*. Nijmegen.

Giannelli, C. (1950). *Bybliothecae Apostolicae Vaticanae codices manu scripti recensiti Vaticani graeci* (1485-1683). Roma.

―――― (1961). *Bybliothecae Apostolicae Vaticanae codices manu scripti recensiti Vaticani graeci* (1684-1744). Roma.

Gollob, E. (1908). Medizinische griechische Handschriften des Jesutien-Kollegiums in Wien. *Sitzungsberichte der Kaiserlichen Akademie der Wissenschaften in Wien, Philosophisch-historische Klasse, 158*, 5. Wien.

Gow, A. S. F. and Scholfield, A. F. (1953). *Nicander, Poems and poetical fragments*. Edited with an English translation. Cambridge University Press.

Hagen (1974). Dietz. In *Altpreußische Biographie, V*, 1. Marburg.

Harlfinger, D. and J. (1974, 1980). *Wasserzeichen aus griechischen Handschriften*, 2 vols. Berlin: Mielke.

Hippocrate, De l'ancienne médecine (1990). Ed. J. Jouanna. Paris.

I.R.H.T. *Guide pour l'élaboration d'une notice de manuscrit* (1977). Prepared by M.-J. Beaud, L. Fossier, et alii. *Institut de recherche et d'histoire des textes, bibliographies, colloques, travaux préparatoires – Série Informatique et Documentation textuelle*. Paris.

―――― *Liste des catalogues des manuscrits grecs parus depuis 1975 mis à la disposition des lecteurs de l'I.R.H.T.* (1986). Paris. Unpublished.

Jemolo, V. and Morelli, M. (Eds.) (1984). *Guida ad una descrizione catalografica uniforme del manoscritto.* Roma.

Kibre, P. (1975-1982). Hippocrates latinus: Repertorium of Hippocratic Writings in the Latin Middle Ages. *Traditio, 31,* 99-126; *32,* 257-292; *33,* 253-295; *34,* 193-226; *35,* 273-302; *36,* 347-372; *37,* 267-289; *38,* 165-192.

Kollesch, J. (1973). Hermann Diels in seiner Bedeutung für die Geschichte der antiken Medizin. *Philologus 117,* 278-283. Berlin and Wiesbaden.

Likhacev, N. P. (1899). *La signification paléographique des filigranes du papier,* 3 v. Saint-Petersburg: V. S. Balasher. In Russian.

Lilla, S. (1985). *Bybliothecae Apostolicae Vaticanae codices manu scripti recensiti Vaticani graeci* (2162-2254). Roma.

Martini, A. and Bassi, D. (1906). *Catalogus codicum graecorum Bibliothecae Ambrosianae.* 2 v. Milano.

Mercati, G. (1938). Pretesi scritti di Paolo l'Egineta e di Galeno and Pretesi scritti di medicina greca. In *Opere minori. Studi e Testi, 78,*3, pp.521-524. Roma.

Mercati, G. and De'Cavalieri, P. F. (1923). *Bybliothecae Apostolicae Vaticanae codices manu scripti recensiti Vaticani graeci,* t. 1. Roma.

Molhuysen, P. C. (1910). *Bibliothecae Universitatis Leidensis. Codices manuscripti 1. Codices Vulcaniani; 2. Codices Scaligeriani.* Leiden.

Monumenta chartae papyraceae historiam illustrantia. (1950 seq.). Hilversum and Amsterdam: Paper Publications.

Mosin, V. A. and Trajlic, S. M. (1957). *Filigranes des XIIIᶜ et XIVᶜ siècles.* 2 vols. Zagreb: Académie Yougoslave des Sciences et des Beaux-Arts, Institut d'Histoire.

The National Library of Medicine. A Summary Checklist of Medical Manuscripts on Microfilm. Bethesda, Maryland, The United States of America.

Pauly, A., Wissowa, G. and Kroll, W. (eds.) (1893 *seq.*). *Realencyklopädie der klassischen Altertumswissenschaft* (1893 seq.). Stuttgart: A. Druckenmüller Verlag.

Revilla, O. A. (1936). *Catalogo de los Codices Griegos de la Biblioteca de El Escorial,* vol. 1. Madrid.

Richard, M. (1958). Répertoire des bibliothèques et des catalogues de manuscrits grecs. *Publications de l'Institut de recherche et d'histoire des textes, 1.* Paris
——— (1964). Répertoire des bibliothèques et des catalogues de manuscrits grecs. Supplément I (1958-1963). *Documents, études et répertoire publiés par l'Institut de recherche et d'histoire des textes, 9.* Paris

Richtlinien Handschriftenkatalogisierung, 4 Auflage (1985). Ed. J. Autenrieth et alii. Bonn.

Riddle, J. M. (1985). *Dioscorides on pharmacy and medicine.* Austin.

Stevenson, H. (1885). *Bybliotheca Apostolica Vaticana . . . Codices manuscripti Palatini Graeci.* Roma.

——— (1888). *Bibliothecae Apostolicae Vaticanae codices manuscripti recensiti . . . codices manuscripti graeci Reginae Suevorum et Pii PP II.* Roma.

Stornajolo, C. (1895). *Bibliothecae Apostolicae Vaticanae codices manuscripti . . . Codices Urbinates graeci . . .* Roma.

Thomson, M. H. (1933). Catalogue des manuscrits grecs de Paris contenant des traités anonymes de botanique. *Revue des études grecques, 46.* Paris.

Touwaide, A. (1981). *Les deux traités de toxicologie attribués à Dioscoride — La tradition manuscrite grecque — Edition critique du texte grec — Traduction et index*, 5 vols. Louvain-la-Neuve.

Wellmann, M. (1907-1914). *Pedanii Dioscuridis Anazarbei, De materia medica libri quinque*, 3 vols. Reprinted 1958. Berlin.

MARC Cataloguing
for Medieval Manuscripts:
An Evaluation

Hope Mayo

SUMMARY. For access to medieval manuscript sources scholars have traditionally relied on hard-copy book-format catalogues. Recently however there has been considerable interest in creating computerized manuscript catalogues or databases of manuscripts, and several innovative if mutually incompatible systems have been developed for this purpose. In the library world, computerized cataloguing systems utilizing the MARC format have been widely used for the past two decades, and databases and networks based on this format offer a well-tested means of communicating bibliographical information. Using two manuscripts from the Huntington Library as

Hope Mayo holds a PhD in medieval history from Harvard University and an MA in Library Science from the University of Chicago. She has published a catalogue of the manuscripts belonging to the Augustiner-Chorherrenstift at Herzogenburg: *Descriptive inventories of manuscripts microfilmed for the Hill Monastic Manuscript Library, Austrian libraries*, vol. III: *Herzogenburg* (Collegeville, MN, 1985), and she served for four years as a member of the Bibliographic Standards Committee of the Rare Books and Manuscripts Section of the Association of College and Research Libraries, American Library Association (ACRL/ALA). She is Associate Curator of Printed Books at The Pierpont Morgan Library, 29 East 36th Street, New York, NY 10016.

In addition to her fellow participants in the Symposium on "Computer Programmes for Medieval and Renaissance Sources," the author would like to thank these colleagues who read and commented on this paper: Anna Lou Ashby, Jackie M. Dooley, M., Consuelo W. Dutschke, Sara Shatford Layne, Alexandra Mason, and Elizabeth O'Keefe. She is also indebted to the Huntington Library and to Consuelo W. Dutschke for permission to reproduce descriptions of Huntington manuscripts HM 64 and HM 1035 and reformat these for the purpose of demonstrating MARC cataloguing.

examples, this paper explores in detail the possibilities and limitations of cataloguing medieval codices in MARC format.

THE MARC FORMAT
AND LIBRARY CATALOGUING

The MAchine-Readable Cataloguing, or MARC, format was developed by the Library of Congress in the 1960s as a communications protocol for the recording and exchange of bibliographic data. At an early date it was adopted by the British National Bibliography and by automated library cataloguing projects in Britain, and it has been utilized subsequently in a number of other countries as the basis for computerized recording of bibliographical information, whether to support library cataloguing or to facilitate the compilation of national or special bibliographies. Although the MARC formats so developed differ somewhat from one another in the details of their application, they are in theory mutually compatible. More recently, the goal of international exchange of bibliographic data has been enhanced by the development of UNIMARC as a mediating format for the conversion of MARC-based records. Furthermore, the foreign marketing efforts of American bibliographic utilities, especially OCLC, seem likely to extend use of the protocols and standards associated with USMARC in its present configuration.

In the United States, most library cataloguing is now done in MARC format. The Library of Congress produces tapes of its cataloguing for current publications, and these are distributed to the bibliographic utilities—the two principal ones are On-line Computer Library Center [OCLC] and Research Libraries Information Network [RLIN]—and to a few large libraries which maintain their own systems. Members of the utilities, who also contribute catalogue records for their holdings not found in the database to which they subscribe, derive records from those supplied by the Library of Congress or other member libraries or create original records using the format. Depending on their local situations, individual libraries then use the utilities to process their own MARC records, producing card sets which are filed in local card catalogues, or Computer Output Microfiche [COM] catalogues, or tapes which are loaded into local on-line catalogues.

The three factors which determine the practical application and results of MARC cataloguing are the format itself, the cataloguing rules used to determine the choice and form of the information entered into the container provided by the format, and the implementation provided by the utility, network, or computer system used to process or give access to the record. The record structure or the format itself consists of three parts: the leader, or data elements that provide information for processing the record; the directory, or series of entries that contain the tag, length, and starting location of each variable field within a record; and the variable fields, which contain the data content of the record, but also some control information.[1] Each element within these three sections is designated by a numerical label or tag; although information recorded in the leader and the directory is used in indexing the record, my discussion of MARC cataloguing for medieval manuscripts will concentrate principally on the definition and content of the variable data fields, of which a summary is supplied for those valid in the USMARC Archives and Manuscript Control format (see Appendix 1). In this list the indented headings indicate major subdivisions of the format according to the type of information recorded in each section, and the individual tags and field titles give a summary indication of the categories of descriptive and indexing information available to the user of a MARC record. Although I have not recorded the details here, each field is further divided into subfields for the more exact definition and distinction of the information recorded, and many are supplied with numerical indicators indicating the type or source of the field content or giving instructions to the system for the processing of the information.[2]

Although it is evident that the choice and definition of tags has some effect on the nature and structure of the information that can be entered into a MARC record or retrieved from it, the form which the data content takes is determined by the cataloguing rules used in conjunction with the format and by the authority structure used to regularize the forms of names and titles entered into the record. At present in the United States these standards are embodied in the second edition of *Anglo-American Cataloging Rules* in the revised reprint of 1988 [AACR2r], which incorporates rules for description, for selecting main and added entries, and for establishing standard forms of personal and corporate names and titles of works. Such names officially established according to AACR2 by the Library of Congress reside in the Library of Congress Name Authority File and are supplemented by headings locally established according to the same standard.[3] For subject cataloguing, unlike descriptive cataloguing, there are no standard or official rules, but in practice most libraries choose subject headings or indexing terms from one of a variety of controlled subject vocabularies, such as the *Library of Congress Subject Headings* [LCSH] or *Medical Subject Headings* [MeSH]. Although the development and implementation of the MARC format in the United States and Britain has taken place in close conjunction with the development of the *Anglo-American Cataloging Rules*, an association seen as a drawback by some potential users of MARC, there is no necessary connection between the format and the cataloguing rules used with it. Nevertheless the uniform application of rules and authorities is essential to efficient and accurate searching and retrieval within a given database; thus because I am most familiar with USMARC and AACR2, I shall use them as the basis for my discussion of the possibilities and limitations of MARC cataloguing for medieval codices. I shall refer later to the development of specialized rules under AACR2 for the better description of certain kinds of material and to the implementation of separate MARC databases for particular categories of books using modified cataloguing rules and non-AACR2 name forms.

Finally, it must be noted that the computer system through which MARC format cataloguing is implemented also affects the results that can be obtained. In the United States the two major bibliographic utilities, RLIN and OCLC, base their systems on the USMARC format and require AACR2 as a standard for the input of current cataloguing, but they differ from each other and from USMARC in some details of implementation and in the products and services they offer their subscribers. I have illustrated this phenomenon by including in the list of variable data tags for USMARC/AMC several fields defined or implemented by RLIN differently from or in addition to the fundamental USMARC standard. More importantly, however, it is the system, whether national bibliographic utility or local on-line catalogue, that determines what fields of a MARC record, and therefore what kinds of information, will be indexed and thus retrievable. For example, fields 655 (Form/Genre) and 755 (Physical Characteristics), the importance of which for medieval manuscript cataloguing in MARC will become apparent, are indexed together by RLIN, not at all by OCLC, and together with subjects and/or added entries by the few on-line catalogues equipped to index them in any way. The computer system may also restrict the maximum length of the record or of individual fields or may limit the total number of fields permitted within a single record. On-line public access catalogues are often supported by programs that place further restrictions on the types of bibliographical information they index and the amount of information they display.

The MARC format was developed for and first applied to the shared cataloguing of modern monographic and serial publications, but it was subsequently extended to cartographic materials (maps and globes), music (both scores and sound recordings), visual materials (two- and three-dimensional objects, still and moving images), computer files, and archives and manuscripts control. The materials in each of these classes have common elements of form or content that differentiate them from each other and that determine the descriptive standards appropriate to each. These are reflected in the chapters of AACR2 that provide special rules for special kinds of materials, and in addition, most specialized user communities have found it appropriate to provide separately published additions to or glosses on the basic AACR2 rules for their format. This is true both of the archives and (modern) manuscripts community and of the cataloguers of early printed books, to name only the two examples most relevant to medieval manuscript cataloguing.

At present in the United States these seven categories of materials correspond to a family of seven formats encompassed within the *USMARC Format for bibliographic data* [UFBD]. Although tag content is fundamentally uniform across the seven formats, some tags are validated for some formats but not for others — see for example field 653 in the list of MARC tags in Appendix 1 — and the subfields or subdivisions of information within tags often differ from format to format depending on the requirements for the type of material being described. Moreover serials and archives and manuscripts control differ from the other formats in that they represent conditions of issue and aspects of control that could be applicable to any type of material. In the United States these inconsistencies will be removed with the implementation in 1993 of format integration, whereby all USMARC tags will be validated for all types of material, each to be used whenever applicable to the item being catalogued. At the same time, the possibility of control based on seriality of issue, on collection-level description, or on the processing history of an item or collection will be extended to all types of material, textual or other.[4] This should bring distinct advantages to cataloguers of older, manuscript, and non-print materials, but for the present a practical discussion of MARC cataloguing for medieval manuscripts must be based on an analysis of the Archives and Manuscripts Control [AMC] format.

ARCHIVES AND MANUSCRIPTS CONTROL

This format was implemented in USMARC in 1984 at the request of and in cooperation with the Society of American Archivists, who had found the previous MARC manuscripts format, which AMC replaced, too closely related to the books format to be suitable for the description of large and growing archival collections or large and heterogeneous collections of modern manuscripts and personal papers (Lytle, 1984). The new format introduced several new and potentially revolutionary characteristics into MARC: provision for collection-level rather than item-level cataloguing; the possibility of linking records at various levels of description, i.e., the possibility of providing separate catalogue records for certain items or subsets of material within a large collection also catalogued as a whole; the availability of extensive note fields; and the possibility of recording the processing history of a collection, particularly important in the case of an actively accumulating archive. Special rules for the description of material in this format were provided in *Archives, personal papers, and manuscripts* [APPM], first published in 1983 and now available in a second edition, which its subtitle describes as "A Cataloging Manual for archival repositories, historical societies, and manuscript libraries" (Hensen, 1989).

As this summary implies, the emphasis in AMC is on collections of modern material. Nevertheless APPM and other guides to cataloguing in AMC tacitly admit the possibility that the format will also be used for cataloguing what one of them refers to as "rare or literary manuscripts" (Sahli, 1985; see examples under fields 130, 510, 520). Thus APPM provides examples for physical descriptions that read "20 leaves: vellum" (APPM 1.5C1), or "1 item (1 leaf): parchment; 35 x 66 cm. folded to 10 x 19 cm." (APPM 1.5D2), and among its sample bibliographical notes it includes: "Listed in: Ricci. *Census*; vol. 1, p. 857, no. 4" (APPM 1.7B14). Similarly chapter 4 of AACR2, which includes basic rules for cataloguing manuscripts, refers to the construction of titles for "Ancient, medieval, and Renaissance manuscripts and oriental manuscripts lacking a title page" (AACR2r 4.1B2) and provides for additional notes describing the style of writing, illustrative matter, collation, other physical details, and opening words of such codices (AACR2r 4.7B23).

MEDIEVAL MANUSCRIPT CATALOGUING

Until now however, there has been little attempt to provide MARC-based cataloguing in any form for pre-1600 manuscripts or documents. A recent search of the RLIN database under the names of common ancient and medieval authors and under the uniform titles prescribed for Bibles and the liturgical books of the Catholic Church yielded, in addition to a few collection-level records, evidence for item-level cataloguing of early manuscripts by only two institutions, Dartmouth College, where the collection appears to consist of leaves and fragments, and Stanford University, RLIN's host institution.

There are undoubtedly various reasons for this situation. In the United States few libraries have any number of medieval manuscripts, nor is much use made of them in most places apart from occasional exhibitions. Curators of American rare book collections seldom have the historical or linguistic training required to deal with medieval materials, and in many smaller academic institutions there are no faculty members with the appropriate specialties. Given this lack of expertise and local interest, together with the pressure of other library needs, it is not surprising that American institutions

have given little attention to the question of manuscript cataloguir
in general. Even so, in recent years a number of libraries have ol
tained or sought to obtain grants to support special projects for tl
cataloguing of their medieval codices, and those curators whom
polled informally in the course of preparing this paper indicated th
they would be happy to have their medieval manuscripts repr(
sented in their MARC systems and on-line catalogues if someor
would develop rules for entering useful descriptions in this forma

This is the crux of the matter. From the scholar's point of viev
students of medieval manuscripts have long relied on hard-cop
catalogues, preferably those published as books, which are con
pletely portable and can be consulted virtually anywhere and und(
any conditions. In the last three decades standards for the compil;
tion of such catalogues have been elaborated which allow the pr(
duction of highly refined and flexible instruments of research. Th
is especially true of the rules and catalogues sponsored by tl
Deutsche Forschungsgemeinschaft, and these standards, togeth(
with the example provided by the catalogues of Neil Ker in Britair
have inspired several recent cataloguing efforts in the U.S.A. Ba
bara Shailor's catalogue of the Beinecke Library manuscripts ;
Yale University, the Huntington Library manuscript catalogue b
Consuelo Dutschke and Richard Rouse, and Paul Saenger's cat;
logue of the Newberry Library manuscripts attain a very high star
dard of description and indexing (Shailor, 1984 *seq.*; Dutschk(
1989; Saenger, 1989), and similar efforts are now underway at Ha
vard University and the University of California, Berkeley.[5] Infol
mation in the detail and of the complexity provided by these cat;
logues is not however easily accommodated in the MARC format (
processed by the kinds of computer programs utilized by America
bibliographic utilities, i.e., programs designed to produce librar
catalogue cards or their facsimiles on a computer screen. With e)
amples borrowed from the Huntington Library catalogue and usin
existing Anglo-American rules and standards for description an
name authorities, I have prepared tagged MARC records for tw
manuscripts in order to demonstrate the application and the limit;
tions of MARC cataloguing for medieval manuscripts; these are s(
out in Appendices 2-9 and are discussed in detail immediately b(
low. For purposes of comparison I have also reproduced the moder

detailed description of each of the two manuscripts recently published by Dutschke, whose traditionally organized cataloguing served as the source of information for my MARC records.

MARC RECORD
FOR A SIMPLE MANUSCRIPT

A manuscript book in the Huntington Library, San Marino, California, designated HM 1035, provides an example of a straightforward manuscript easily catalogued under any system (Appendix 2). It will serve to demonstrate the fundamental organization of a MARC-based catalogue record constructed according to standards current in the United States and will also illustrate a few general but not insolvable problems encountered in adapting medieval manuscript cataloguing to this system (see Appendix 3). Since HM 1035 contains three works by Aristotle, the MARC record has a main entry field [100] for the author's name. The title field [245], which for a printed book would be based on the title page, here transcribes the titulus of the first text page of the codex; under other circumstances or even here it would be possible to take this information from the colophon. In either case the source of the title must be stated, as in the note "Caption title from f. 1r." "Caption title" is standard Anglo-American cataloguing terminology for this situation.

For a manuscript the publication and distribution or imprint field [260] may contain only a date, here formulated somewhat awkwardly for scholars accustomed to reading and saying "second half of the thirteenth century"; the brackets are required since this date does not appear in the manuscript itself. According to the existing cataloguing rules for manuscripts, the place of origin of the manuscript must be entered in a note if it is to be recorded (AACR2r 4.7B8; cf. AACR2r 4.4). The format itself accommodates both place and date as well as the name of the publisher for printed materials in field 260, and the rules for printed books instruct that these elements be recorded in this area of the cataloguing record. It would seem logical to modify the rules for manuscripts so as to permit the inclusion here of both place and date for medieval codices. In most existing MARC systems neither place nor date of origin is indexed directly; but this is a question of systems implementation, and the problem can be circumvented by re-entering these data elements in indexed local fields. Place may also be indexed in field 752 with a hierarchical entry, i.e., an entry under the modern name of the country of origin, subdivided by region or city.

Field 300 includes the fundamental description of the extent of the manuscript, together with some features of its material and format (number of columns and lines, material), but omits details of flyleaves, which are usually included in traditional statements of extent.[6] The measurement, 37 cm., approximating the height of the binding, is so abbreviated as to say virtually nothing of interest to scholars, but it would be easy to include the full dimensions of leaf size and written area at this point. Other physical characteristics — script, decoration, collation, catchwords, signatures, ruling, pricking, and other features — must be described in notes [500]. If this information is to be indexed in most existing MARC systems, this must be done by using field 755, defined for "Added Entry — Physical Characteristics," which however accommodates only controlled indexing vocabulary taken from approved lists that have source codes assigned by the Library of Congress. Although I have assigned terms from existing thesauri for *Binding Terms* (1988) and *Provenance Evidence* (1988) by way of example, there is at present no approved English-language list which provides terms that apply specifically to medieval manuscripts. Free-text searching of note fields would of course give direct access to this information, but this capability is system-dependent and introduces the problems of retrieval always occasioned by searching in a situation where vocabularies are not controlled.

Detailed information as to the contents of the codex and its origin and provenance must also be given in notes, some of which have specially assigned MARC tags reflecting the kind of information reported in them. This information too — the names of authors and translators; the titles of individual works; the genres represented and subjects treated; the names of previous owners; the names of scribes and artists when known — must be repeated in standardized form in fields of the 6XX or 7XX blocks of the record if it is to be indexed directly by existing MARC systems.

In the MARC cataloguing record for HM 1035, the individual

works in the manuscript are indexed with author and title in field 700, and the titles could have been indexed separately in field 740, were this desired. I did not include or index incipits for this manuscript but shall discuss below the particular problems posed by incipits in the context of MARC cataloguing. Two Library of Congress subject headings, "Animals" and "Zoology—Pre-Linnean works," are included in this record because the MARC-based bibliographic utilities require the inclusion of at least one subject heading in each full cataloguing record entered in their databases (Mayo, 1990). Following the tagged MARC record for HM 1035, there is a formatted version of the description without MARC tags, in order to demonstrate what the catalogue record might look like after processing by a bibliographic utility (see Appendix 4).

The limitations on indexing, the need to take subject headings from an established list (here LCSH), and the requirement that names and titles be standardized according to rules developed primarily by and for cataloguers of modern publications will appear as onerous conditions to some. Nevertheless even within these constraints it is possible to construct a MARC record that includes most essential points of description and access for a manuscript such as HM 1035, which is characterized by the orderly presentation of identifiable works. Where detailed description or specialized indexing of information particularly interesting to medievalists is not at present available, most of these deficiencies could be made good by system-provided free-text searching, by slightly modifying the existing cataloguing rules, and by authorizing a thesaurus of terms for the description of medieval manuscripts.

MULTI-LEVEL CATALOGUING
FOR A COMPLEX MANUSCRIPT

Another medieval codex from the Huntington Library, HM 64, is intellectually and physically a very complex manuscript (see Appendix 5) and one whose practical and anonymous astronomical and medical texts are likely to be of much greater interest to historians of science than HM 1035's copy of Aristotle on animals. Since the codex represents no one or even a principal author, it must be entered under title; fortunately the existing rules for *Archives, personal papers, and manuscripts* (Hensen, 1989) allow the creation of a title for a collection of materials, a principle easily expanded to cover a compilation such as this one. I have entered it under the title provided in the published Huntington Library catalogue, but this is in fact no more than a subject summary which gives no specific access to the contents of the manuscript. As the published description clearly shows, this codex contains many relatively short, often anonymous, texts and a number of tables and diagrams, sometimes with explanatory text. A few of them can be identified by author and title or by citing the source from which they were excerpted or translated, although the modern attribution is often not that given in the manuscript itself. Others are identified by reference to published lists of incipits — Thorndike-Kibre (rev. ed. 1963) or the *Index of Middle English Verse* (Brown and Robbins, 1943; Robbins and Cutler, 1965) for example — or to specialized articles, or simply by their incipits and the cataloguer's characterization of the text. Recipes and charms, always a problem for the cataloguer, are described only in groups according to their locations in the manuscript, languages, and principal subjects. Each of the 57 text units identified in the published description of the manuscript is characterized by some combination of these types of information. Although many of these units are themselves complex in content, the relation among the various points of information provided in each is made quite clear by the format of the description as it progresses through the manuscript section by section.

Such logical linking of various types of information in varying combinations is not possible in a MARC record as its fields are currently structured. Instead, contents information and citations are listed separately within the notes area of the record. The MARC format provides for a field, structured formally [505] or informally [500], which itemizes the contents of the item catalogued, but supposes that this information will be taken from or made to approximate the chapter list of a table of contents or the titles of volumes in a set. In the AMC format and the special rules for it, there is provision for a field [351] which summarizes the organization of an archival or manuscript collection by identifying and explaining the arrangement of series and subseries within it, and there is a note field [520] which accommodates a narrative summary of the contents of the collection. For HM 64 I have used the information in the published description to create what is by library standards a very long and detailed summary or contents note—an informal one in MARC's terms, since the manuscript contains no table of contents to transcribe; this note appears in the tagged record divided among three long 500 fields because most systems limit the length of a single field to the amount of text that can be displayed on one computer screen (see Appendices 6 and 7). Since the content or summary field is the only place in a MARC record where the entire intellectual organization of a manuscript can be systematically displayed, I have gone beyond the mandates of the existing cataloguing codes and have linked the individual items in the contents note with the more detailed description of the published catalogue by including the item numbers preceding each section, and I have provided direct references to the manuscript itself by giving the inclusive foliation in parentheses after each title. Within this structure however, the type of summary contents information I was able to supply varies from unit to unit: some have true titles, whether present in the manuscript or supplied by the cataloguer; most have made-up titles created for the published description or constructed by me on the basis of Dutschke's summary; and in several cases (indicated here by bold type) only an incipit was available to designate the content of a section. Not only is the choice of information necessarily inconsistent; I have summarized brutally in instance after instance where the multiple tituli, incipits, citations, and descriptive summaries provided in single sections of the published description show how complex the material is and how much summarizing has already taken place.

In situations where a work has no identifiable author or established title, the medievalist relies for identification on the incipit or on a reference to a published repertory of texts, but MARC format cataloguing does not accommodate these types of information in the juxtaposition required by the scholar. Citations in the MARC format are given in a separate, repeatable note field [510] which effectively separates them from the text to which they refer. In some systems field 510 is directly searchable, and this gives MARC records an advantage over traditional manuscript catalogues in which citations are rarely indexed. But neither the cataloguing rules nor the format provides a ready way of distinguishing within a single record between citations which refer to the manuscript as a whole and those which apply to a single text within it.

With regard to incipits, the *Anglo-American Cataloging Rules* prefer titles supplied by the cataloguer to title-substitutes created by quoting the opening words of a text. Although the special rules for rare book cataloguing allow the use of the opening words in place of a title when no title can be found in the item being catalogued, the existing rules for manuscripts provide for the transcription of incipits only when and only after the title of the text has been supplied by the cataloguer, and they instruct that incipits be given as general notes separate from the contents note. Thus, when the cataloguer wishes to give both a supplied title and a true incipit, a very common situation in medieval manuscript cataloguing, the MARC format requires that these two elements be reported separately. Furthermore if incipits are to be indexed, they must be repeated in the 740 field, which is provided for the tracing of related and variant titles. That field however was not intended to accommodate this type or amount of title information.

The MARC format does offer a linking mechanism for relating the information which refers to a particular part of a record to the material to which it applies, in that certain fields may open with subfield §3, containing text that identifies the related material. For HM 64 in the version of the record designated "partial" (see Appendix 6), I have provided a selection of citation notes in 510 fields, each linked by subfield §3 to the appropriate numbered item in the general contents note; but even with this help, it is impossible to visualize clearly the connections between citations and the texts to which they apply. Likewise I have provided a sampling of field 500 notes giving incipits and similarly linked by subfield §3 to specific items in the contents note; the result is a similar confusion. To use this technique for recording and indexing all the incipits reported in the printed description would result moreover in the creation of a very long record. Because of these defects, this sample record does not offer a satisfactory representation of the information and the relationships so clearly conveyed in the traditionally formatted published description of HM 64. In short, the full complexity of a manuscript such as this one cannot be conveyed comprehensibly in a single MARC record which takes into account the present restrictions of the format and which follows cataloguing rules developed with reference to printed books or modern manuscripts.

With HM 64, the fundamental difficulty is that the MARC format provides no way of combining in the same field any or all of these elements for the individual texts contained within a codex: author, title (whether from the manuscript or supplied by the cataloguer), incipit(s), and citation(s); any or all of these may be significant for the identification of the text, and their linkage is particularly important for this purpose. To this difficulty there are at present two possible solutions. One is to avoid the problem by creating a summary record in which the contents note mentions only types of material and a few specific texts where clear identification by author or title is possible. These and these alone are indexed in the appropriate indexing fields, and access to the record is via a relatively few authors, titles, subjects, types of works, or physical characteristics. In this case the MARC record performs a true census function, guiding the scholar to a fuller published or in-house description which alone contains much of the information needed for detailed research.[7]

A second solution lies in multi-level cataloguing, a technique by which a parent record for the whole manuscript is linked to separate records for each of the individual text units within it. The general title, the physical description and history of the entire codex, a summary account of its contents, and the citations referring to the manuscript as a whole reside in this record. The separate records for each unit describe and index the author, title, subjects, and citations for that unit, as applicable; and these records are linked with the parent record by the presence in each of a linking field which cites the main entry of the parent record and its record number within a particular database. I have demonstrated the application of this technique to HM 64 in the record designated "parent" and the two records designated "component part." The parent record contains the complete contents listing, the physical description of the codex, citations to general descriptions of it, an account of its history, and the indexing for these aspects (see Appendix 7). Of the component parts, the record for item 17 by Bartholomeus de Ferraria illustrates the cataloguing of a section that consists of continuous identifiable text, but also one that is misattributed in the manuscript and there-fore one whose accurate identification depends on references to a published repertory (see Appendix 8). Conversely the record for item 16, identified as "charms," illustrates the case of a part that consists of miscellaneous similar but anonymous texts for which the incipits provide the only accurate designations or access points (see Appendix 9). Each component part record focuses exclusively on the description of that part of the manuscript; each is able to record and index incipits while remaining reasonable in length; and the record for the charms demonstrates a comprehensible use of the subfield §3 linking mechanism.

Although this paper is concerned principally with the cataloguing of texts found in manuscripts, it is appropriate at this point to re-mark that the multi-level approach to cataloguing complex manu-scripts can also be applied to the cataloguing of images within man-uscripts. The question of how to describe images and how to record this information in computerized form is one that is being addressed by a number of art indexing projects which have adopted a variety of solutions to problems, such as choice of terminology, that I can-not discuss here. I should like however to remark that the Index of Medieval Medical Images [IMMI], based at the University of Cali-fornia at Los Angeles, has adopted the MARC Visual Materials format for the purpose of describing individual medical images found in medieval manuscripts – including, as it happens, HM 64. In this approach identification and description of the image take precedence in the record, in that a descriptive title for the image appears as the heading [245] and a detailed description of the con-tent of the picture in a summary note [520]. The record also in-cludes a brief physical description of the image, indexing by subject and genre, and references to the place and date of origin and to the present location and identification of the parent manuscript. In a system based on multi-level cataloguing for manuscripts and their component parts, records for individual images could be linked to the parent record describing the entire manuscript in the same way as component-part records for the individual texts within the codex. Describing and indexing miniatures and drawings in this way would render accessible in a single context aspects of manuscripts that are often inadequately represented in traditional text-oriented manu-script catalogues.[8]

The multi-level approach to the cataloguing of a complex manuscript has the advantage of allowing the more detailed description of individual units within the manuscript; it separates specific from general citations and references; and it solves the problem of linking the various kinds of information about a single text or image. To the medievalist it has two chief disadvantages: for information about the codex as a whole it is necessary to refer to the parent record, and what is more significant, the allocation of the contents descriptions to separate records—in the case of HM 64, as many as 57 of them for the component texts alone—makes it extremely difficult to envision the manuscript as an intellectual whole. While the length of the individual catalogue records is reduced, cataloguers of modern material and those responsible for systems implementation may object to the proliferation of records relating to what appears to them a single book and to the seeming duplication of information that will occur if each unit of some manuscripts is catalogued separately: envision for example the very similar records that would result from describing and indexing the various sections of recipes in HM 64.

ASSESSMENT:
PROBLEMS AND POSSIBILITIES

On the basis of this summary discussion of sample MARC records for HM 1035 and HM 64, it is possible to make a preliminary assessment of the problems of MARC cataloguing for medieval manuscripts. Use of the USMARC format and the *Anglo-American Cataloging Rules* produces descriptions which can replicate many of the basic features of traditional manuscript descriptions, but these are organized differently from the published descriptions to which scholars are accustomed. In the MARC format, emphasis is on primary access to the manuscript through the author of its principal text or under a summary title; detailed contents information, incipits, citations, physical description, and provenance information are placed in notes where this information appears in a more or less unfamiliar order and is not indexed directly, as one might expect in an on-line environment. Systematic description of and access to individual parts of complex manuscripts is possible only through a mechanism whereby separate on-line records are created for the individual texts and linked to a parent record containing the general description of the manuscript as a whole. The names of authors and the formulation of uniform titles often take, or are indexed under, unfamiliar forms. The physical characteristics of a manuscript book (whether codicological, paleographical, or decorative) and the genres and subjects of texts, although they can be described in detail in the notes, are indexed primarily through the use of controlled vocabulary from approved lists. Of the approved lists which are available, the *Library of Congress Subject Headings* are frequently too general to be ideally applicable in a specialized context; and other potentially useful lists, such as *Medical Subject Headings*, use terms that reflect modern medical knowledge and no longer correspond to the medieval world view or medieval medical terminology. As yet there exist no specialized thesauri for indexing the genres of works represented in medieval manuscripts or the physical characteristics of medieval codices. Furthermore there is no adequate provision for the reporting or indexing of incipits, since the *Anglo-American Cataloging Rules* as presently written prefer cataloguer-supplied titles to de facto titles created by transcribing the first words of the text. Incipits are thus admitted only as a last resort; the rules give no instructions for tracing them but indicate in general that supplied titles are not to be indexed.[9] Last but not least, there is no generally applicable provision for indexing what AACR2 calls the repository designation; although popular names of manuscripts may be indexed as alternate titles, the familiar and unique designation consisting of library, collection if applicable, and shelfmark is not considered appropriate for this purpose if the manuscript or its content can be designated by any other means.

Of these limitations the only one inherent in the structure of the MARC format as presently defined in the United States is the limitation on complex linking of author, title, incipit, and reference within the same record; and the solution to this problem, involving the use of multiple linked records, in fact has the potential of allowing the clear organization and indexing of a greater amount of descriptive information. Other limitations related to current implementations of the format, but not inherent in its structure, are the failure to index directly place and date of origin and the emphasis on controlled indexing vocabulary, whether in standardized forms of names and titles or in the selection of other indexing terms from approved lists. All the other limitations described, including the forms of names and titles actually selected, are primarily functions of the *Anglo-American Cataloging Rules*.

PRECEDENTS FOR MARC CATALOGUING OF SPECIAL MATERIALS

How can these problems be resolved, and to what extent is resolution possible? Two different approaches to MARC-based cataloguing of special materials offer instructive precedents for considering these questions with regard to medieval manuscripts. I have briefly outlined the history of the Archives and Manuscript Control format and the development of its rules. Long before this, as the viability of MARC format for computerizing bibliographic records for current publications began to be demonstrated by experience, as the library world committed itself to machine cataloguing, and as databases of modern materials increased in size and usefulness, interest grew in applying MARC format cataloguing to older printed books. The history of this effort need not be told in full here, but its results are of interest for medieval manuscript cataloguing in MARC. Since the accurate cataloguing of early printed books requires exact title page transcription, sometimes including original punctuation, and since the edition and imprint statements of early printed books may be formulated or located differently from those of their modern counterparts, the Library of Congress developed a special set of rules for the *Bibliographic description of rare books* [BDRB, 1981] which combined traditional descriptive standards with ISBD punctuation under the general directives of AACR2. And since the identification of genres of works and the description of copy-specific characteristics of individual books are far more important to the complete cataloguing of early printed or rare books than they are in the case of modern trade editions, two additional fields were validated in the MARC format: 655 for the indexing of form and genre as distinct from subject; and 755 for description and indexing of physical characteristics. Only terms from approved thesauri may used in these fields, and a number of such lists have been developed by the American rare book community or by other cataloguers of special materials.[10]

Other significant precedents for machine cataloguing of early materials lie in two projects whose home is at the British Library: the Eighteenth-century Short Title Catalogue [ESTC], and the Incunable Short Title Catalogue [ISTC]. ESTC began in the late 1970s and has as its object the census and recording of all works in any language published in the eighteenth century in the English-speaking areas of the world and all works in English published anywhere in the world during the same period (Alston and Jannetta, 1978). Despite its name of "short title catalogue," it provides extensive title page transcriptions and reports copy-specific characteristics and variations. Its importance in the context of this discussion is that it was a computerized MARC-based project from the beginning; it developed its own cataloguing rules which retained many features of traditional descriptive bibliographic practices; and its results, though accessible through the general on-line catalogue at the British Library, reside in RLIN in a special database which allows it to maintain its distinctive features.

In contrast, ISTC was begun at the British Library by keyboarding Frederick R. Goff's *Incunabula in American libraries* (Goff, 1964; Goff, 1973) and by adding to this information from the incunable catalogues of the British Library and some other European institutions (Hellinga and Goldfinch, 1987). ISTC's records are not based on direct inspection of the books; though a census of locations, it contains little copy-specific descriptive information (a point that has been criticized); its name forms and uniform titles and its formulation of imprint information differ from AACR2 standards; and although it uses MARC tags in their generally accepted significations, it permits variations which no general bibliographic utility is equipped to accommodate, e.g., the repetition of MARC 260 (the imprint field) when the attribution of an early edition is uncertain or disputed. How these variations will be handled when ISTC is incorporated into the RLIN Books File remains to be seen.

A third and more radical solution to the problem of adapting MARC to medieval manuscripts is implied in the article *A MARC-Format for Mediaeval Codices* (Corthouts, 1987). I do not know whether any attempt has been made to implement this format or whether there is explanatory material or documentation for it that was not included in the article. In its published form, consisting only of a list of field tags and titles, this format gives evidence of a thorough understanding of and careful provision for all the special characteristics which must be described and indexed in the ideal catalogue entry for a medieval manuscript. In attaining this level of description however, it reassigns a great many field definitions; e.g., MARC 260, normally defined as "Publication, distribution, etc." — and quite usable for the parallel function of recording the place and date of origin of a codex — becomes "Added entry: personal name in relation to archeology of the codex." Because of these changes this format could be implemented only in a stand-alone system or independent network; it could not be used to integrate medieval manuscript cataloguing into a larger bibliographic context, which should in fact be the point of developing rules and standards for fitting medieval manuscript descriptions into the MARC format and existing databases.

MARC AND MEDIEVAL MANUSCRIPTS

I have spoken within the context of the USMARC format and the *Anglo-American Cataloging Rules* because, although this by no means exhausts the theoretical possibilities of MARC cataloguing for medieval manuscripts, it provides a real context for a preliminary discussion. To customize format and records is expensive and renders the information so organized relatively inaccessible, at least in the United States; this is in fact the principle reason why ISTC records will be integrated into the Books File of the general RLIN database, rather than constituting a special RLIN database, as has been the case with ESTC. The experience of American special materials cataloguers indicates that it is better to work within the existing context, relying on the bibliographic networks for technical support and communication. They have also found that to a considerable extent, not fully explored here, cataloguing and retrieval can be customized even within the context of generally applicable rules and standard implementations of the MARC format. Furthermore as technologies improve, it will become increasingly feasible to download and enhance records in a local system or to link the MARC format description of a manuscript with a local computerized record containing additional information, however organized. Linkage between MARC records and videodisc representations of the items catalogued is already possible, suggesting the application of this technology to the cataloguing of medieval manuscripts and the images they contain.[11]

From the point of view of description and indexing, there exist precedents for the development of specialized rules as supplements to AACR2 and of topical thesauri for indexing special materials or features. Here the experience of the American rare book community provides a useful and workable model, demonstrating that even within the existing limitations of the *Anglo-American Cataloging Rules* it should be feasible to draw up a set of specialized rules, with examples, which would address themselves to the common problems encountered in cataloguing medieval texts in medieval copies and thus provide guidance for fitting most of the information expected by medievalists into the forms required by the rules. I have already referred to the possibility of developing a specialized thesaurus for the description of physical characteristics of manuscripts, and a useful prototype for such a list already exists in Denis Muzerelle's French-language *Vocabulaire codicologique* (1985).

Obtaining alterations in the fundamental cataloguing code or in the format itself are more difficult matters, although it ought to be possible to make a case for always recording and indexing the repository designation, a fundamental identifier that should be applied without exception to the record for a manuscript or any part of it. Although Anglo-American name forms seem strange if not wrong to many medievalists, it will probably be necessary for Americans at least to become accustomed to them. After all most scholars are already walking name authority files, each having learned early in life that names are invariably construed, spelt, and filed differently in different catalogues, indexes, and libraries. What the *Anglo-American Cataloging Rules*, the USMARC format, or the existing bibliographic databases may never be willing or able to accommodate is the extensive recording and indexing of incipits, important as these are to the research needs of medieval scholars. If incipits are to be extensively recorded and indexed in MARC, special tags will probably need to be designated for this purpose.

Most fundamentally, as will have become apparent from my reformulation into MARC of two descriptions from the new Huntington Library catalogue, MARC format cataloguing under the restrictions I have assumed will not accommodate all the fine points of information and detailed discussion of evidence that one expects to find in the best traditional manuscript descriptions. It may be therefore that if MARC-based descriptions of medieval manuscripts reside in general databases they will always have to be regarded as summary or census records. There is already a precedent for this, in that the rules for *Archives, personal papers, and manuscripts* assume that the principal source of information for a MARC record will be the finding aid for the collection being described and that the AMC record will serve as a summary of and an index to this more detailed document, which may be published or not.

In the United States at least, developing MARC records for medieval manuscripts would offer many advantages. Libraries with a variety of types of material, many of them already controlled through MARC format cataloguing, would be able to integrate their medieval manuscript holdings into the same database and on-line catalogue that provide access to the remainder of the collection. Many university libraries are already in a position, resulting from their investment in a bibliographic utility and a local on-line catalogue, to benefit from this development. More importantly, as records for medieval manuscripts are added to the national databases maintained by the bibliographic utilities, the collective information made available will approximate more and more to an update of the *Census of medieval and renaissance manuscripts in the United States and Canada*, first published in 1935-37 and revised only once in a hard copy supplement issued in 1962 (De Ricci and Wilson, 1935; Faye and Bond, 1962). Updating the census is an undertaking that long ago became unimaginable using any traditional means of compilation, and it is a task that would still require massive support for planning, data collection and entry, and database maintenance if it were to be attempted in the context of an independent computerized system. While MARC format cataloguing through the existing bibliographic utilities would not solve all these problems — persons skilled in medieval manuscript studies and library systems would still be required to collect the data and enter it — this technique would utilize existing and well-tried systems for maintenance and communication and would allow institutions and scholars to concentrate on the collection and organization of the data, while upgrading most existing descriptions and disseminating information about manuscripts, their contents, and their locations. Such an approach is perhaps of less interest in Europe where sophisticated standards have been developed for the scholarly description of medieval manuscripts, where large cataloguing projects may already be underway with or without computer assistance, and where national governments recognize the importance of funding efforts to survey and render intellectually accessible the large collections of manuscripts which form an important part of their national patrimonies. Nevertheless MARC's potential as a communications protocol for which forms and procedures are well established is one that should be kept in mind, especially for the compilation of topical and/or supra-national databases. Should a decision be made in favor of a specialized, independent, ESTC-like database, there would be considerable scope for adapting standards of description and indexing to the needs of the project, while maintaining the fundamental structure of the format and thus its potential compatibility with other MARC systems.

NOTES

1. The MARC record structure is an implementation of the *American National Standard Format for Bibliographic Information Interchange on Magnetic Tape* (1971) [ANSI Z39.2-1971], documented in *USMARC Specifications* (1987).

2. The complete official documentation for field and subfield definition is *USMARC Format for Bibliographic Data* (1988) [UFBD]. Each of the bibliographic utilities publishes a supplement to UFBD giving the details of its own implementation of the format, for example *RLIN Supplement* (April 1990). Crawford (1989) provides a general introduction to the format. In this paper and its appendices, MARC fields are referred to by their three-digit numerical tags, indicators are given their appropriate values, and subfield codes (which may be letters or numbers) are identified by the symbol §.

3. NACO, the National Coordinated Cataloging Operations project, formerly the Name Authority Cooperative Project, allows its member libraries to contribute authority records to the Library of Congress Name Authority File; see, e.g., *LC Information Bulletin*, January 15, 1988.

4. In some cases tags will be changed to make definitions consistent. These changes are summarized in *Format Integration* (1988).

5. Two additional catalogues, recently begun at the Walters Gallery (Randall, 1989 seq.) and the Library of Congress (Schutzner, 1989 seq.) have adopted

emphases and formats for description that differ somewhat from the *de facto* standard set by Shailor, Dutschke, and Saenger under the tutelage of R. H. Rouse, but these catalogues too offer a wealth of information to the scholar.

6. See Dutschke: ff.i (early modern paper) + 98 + i (early modern paper).

7. There is precedent for this approach, as there is for using the published description as the principal source of information, in APPM1 4.0B1 which instructs that "the chief source of information for collections of manuscripts and archival records is the finding aid prepared for those materials" (APPM2 1.0B1 refers here to "archival materials").

8. I owe this information about IMMI to Sara Shatford Layne, cataloguing adviser to the project, which is under the direction of Ynez Violé O'Neill. The *IMMI Newsletter* (available from Prof. O'Neill, Medical History Division, Department of Anatomy and Cell Biology, UCLA School of Medicine, Los Angeles, CA 90024, U.S.A.) provides periodic updates on the work of the project.

9. Titles supplied in field 245 are indexed in RLIN and OCLC because this field is always indexed in these on-line systems. However the rule implies that these titles are not to be traced separately, e.g., in field 740, or in off-line catalogues.

10. On the development of descriptors for form, genre, and physical characteristics and the applications of these concepts, see Zinkham, Cloud, and Mayo (1989); Dooley and Zinkham (1990). For brief accounts of recent efforts to create cataloguing standards for rare books, see Davis (1987) and Thomas (1987).

11. Columbia University's AVIADOR, the Avery Videodisc Index of Architectural Drawings on RLIN, uses MARC records that allow searches by architects, titles, building names, and geographic locations to access videodisc reproductions of drawings in the Avery Architectural and Fine Arts Library; see *College & Research Library News*, 51, no. 5 (May 1990) 466.

REFERENCES

Abbreviations

AACR	Anglo-American Cataloging Rules (AACR2 = second edition; AACR2r = second edition revised)
ACRL	Association of College and Research Libraries, a division of ALA
ALA	American Library Association
AMC	Archives and Manuscript Control format of USMARC
ANSI	American National Standards Institute
APPM	Archives, Personal Papers, and Manuscripts (Hensen, 1989: APPM1 = first edition; APPM2 = second edition)
BDRB	Bibliographic Description of Rare Books of the Library of Congress
COM	Computer Output Microfiche
ESTC	Eighteenth-century Short Title Catalogue

HM	The Huntington Library, San Marino, California, Huntington Manuscripts
IMMI	Index of Medieval Medical Images
ISTC	Incunable Short Title Catalogue
LC	Library of Congress, Washington, D.C.
LCSH	Library of Congress Subject Headings
MARC	Machine Readable Cataloguing format
MeSH	Medical Subject Headings
NACO	National Coordinated Cataloging Operations project of LC
OCLC	On-line Computer Library Center, Dublin, Ohio
RBMS	Rare Books and Manuscripts Section of ACRL/ALA
RLIN	Research Libraries Information Network, Stanford University, California
UFBD	USMARC Format for Bibliographic Data
UNIMARC	Format for conversion of MARC-based records
USMARC	MARC as used by LC, OCLC, and RLIN

WORKS CITED

Alston, R. C. and Jannetta, M. J. (1978). *Bibliography, Machine Readable Cataloguing and the ESTC*. London: The British Library.

American National Standard Format for Bibliographic Information Interchange on Magnetic Tape (1971). New York: American National Standards Institute. [ANSI Z39.2-1971].

Anglo-American Cataloging Rules. 2nd edition revised (1988). Chicago: American Library Association.

Bibliographic Description of Rare Books: Rules Formulated Under AACR2 and ISBD(A) for the Descriptive Cataloging of Rare Books and Other Special Printed Materials (1981). Washington, D.C.: Library of Congress. A second revised edition is in preparation.

Binding Terms: A Thesaurus for Use in Rare Book and Special Collections Cataloguing (1988). Prepared by the Standards Committee of the Rare Books and Manuscripts Section (ACRL/ALA). Chicago: Association of College and Research Libraries.

Brown, C. and Robbins, R. H. (1943). *The Index of Middle English Verse*. New York: Printed for the Index Society by the Columbia University Press.

Corthouts, J. (1987). A MARC-format for mediaeval codices. In *Gazette du livre médiéval 11*, 13-17.

Crawford, W. (1989). *MARC for Library Use*. Second edition. Boston: G. K. Hall.

Davis, S. P. (1987). Bibliographic control of special collections: issues and trends. In Michèle Valerie Cloonan (Ed.), *Recent Trends in Rare Book Librarianship in Library Trends 36*, (1) 109-124.

De Ricci, S. and Wilson, W. J. (1935). *Census of Medieval and Renaissance*

Manuscripts in the United States and Canada. New York: The H. W. Wilson Company. Reprinted, New York: H. P. Kraus Reprints, 1961.

Dooley, J. and Zinkham, H. (1990). The object as "subject": providing access to genres, forms of material, and physical characteristics. Forthcoming in *Extending MARC Beyond the Book*. Boston: G. K. Hall.

Dutschke, C. W. (1989). *Guide to Medieval and Renaissance Manuscripts in the Huntington Library*. With the assistance of R. H. Rouse *et alii*. San Marino, Calif.: Huntington Library.

Faye, C. U. and Bond, W. H. (1962). (Edts.). *Supplement to the Census of Medieval and Renaissance Manuscripts in the United States and Canada*. New York: The Bibliographical Society of America.

Format Integration and Its Effect on the USMARC Bibliographic Format (1988). Prepared by Network Development and MARC Standards Office. Washington, D.C.: Cataloging Distribution Service, Library of Congress.

Goff, F. R. (1964). *Incunabula in American Libraries: A Third Census of Fifteenth-Century Books Recorded in North American Collections*. New York: The Bibliographical Society of America.

———— (1973). *Supplement to Incunabula in American Libraries*. New York: The Bibliographical Society of America.

Hellinga, L. and Goldfinch, J. (Eds.). (1987). *Bibliography and the Study of 15th-Century Civilisation: Papers Presented at a Colloquium at the British Library 26-28 September 1984*. London: The British Library.

Hensen, S. L. (1989). *Archives, Personal Papers and Manuscripts: A Cataloging Manual for Archival Repositories, Historical Societies, and Manuscript Libraries*. 1st edition (1983). 2nd edition (1989). Chicago: Society of American Archivists.

Library of Congress Subject Headings. 11th edition (1988). Washington, D.C.: Cataloging Distribution Service, Library of Congress.

Lytle, R. H. (1984). "An Analysis of the work of the National Information Systems Task Force." In *American Archivist 47*, 357-365.

Mayo, H. (1990). Standards for Description, Indexing, and Retrieval in Computerized Catalogs of Medieval Manuscripts. In M. Folkerts and A. Kühne (Eds.), The Use of Computers in Medieval Manuscript Cataloguing: Papers from the International Workshop in Munich, 10-12 August 1989. In *Algorismus 4*. München: Institut für Geschichte der Naturwissenschaften, Universität München.

Medical Subject Headings—Annotated Alphabetic List 1990 (1989). Bethesda, Md.: National Library of Medicine.

Muzerelle, D. (1985). *Vocabulaire Codicologique: Répertoire Méthodique des Termes Français Relatifs aux Manuscrits*. Paris: Éditions CEMI.

Provenance Evidence: Thesaurus for Use in Rare Book and Special Collections Cataloguing (1988). Prepared by the Standards Committee of the Rare Books and Manuscripts Section (ACRL/ALA). Chicago: Association of College and Research Libraries.

Randall, L. (1989 *seq.*). *Medieval and Renaissance Manuscripts in the Walters Art Gallery*. Baltimore: The Johns Hopkins University Press.

RLIN Supplement to USMARC Bibliographic Format (April 1990). Stanford, Calif.: The Research Libraries Group, Inc.

Robbins, R. H. and Cutler, J. L. (1965). *Supplement to the Index of Middle English Verse*. Lexington, Ky.: University of Kentucky Press.

Saenger, P. (1989). *A Catalogue of the Pre-1500 Western Manuscript Books at the Newberry Library*. Chicago: University of Chicago Press.

Sahli, N. (1985). *MARC for Archives and Manuscripts: The AMC Format*. Chicago: The Society of American Archivists.

Schutzner, S. (1989 *seq.*). *Medieval and Renaissance Manuscript Books in the Library of Congress: A Descriptive Catalog*. Washington, D.C.: Library of Congress.

Shailor, B. A. (1984 *seq.*). *Catalogue of Medieval and Renaissance Manuscripts in the Beinecke Rare Book and Manuscript Library, Yale University*. Binghamton, N.Y.: Medieval & Renaissance Texts & Studies.

Thomas, J. B. III (1987). The necessity of standards in an automated environment. In Michèle Valerie Cloonan (Ed.), *Recent Trends in Rare Book Librarianship* in *Library Trends 36*, (1) 125-139.

Thorndike, L. and Kibre, P. (1963). *A Catalogue of Incipits of Mediaeval Scientific Writings in Latin*. Revised and augmented edition. Cambridge, Mass.: Medieval Academy of America.

USMARC Format for Bibliographic Data Including Guidelines for Content Designation (1988). Prepared by Network Development and MARC Standards Office. Washington, D.C.: Cataloging Distribution Service, Library of Congress.

USMARC Specifications for Record Structure, Character Sets, Tapes (1987). Prepared by Network Development and MARC Standards Office. Washington, D.C.: Cataloging Distribution Service, Library of Congress.

Zinkham, H., Cloud, P. D., and Mayo, H. (1989). Providing access by form of material, genre, and physical characteristics: benefits and techniques. In *American Archivist 52*, 300-319.

APPENDIX 1.

USMARC AMC—
VARIABLE DATA FIELDS

[Based on UFBD (1988), and RLIN Supplement (April 1990).]

1XX Main Entries

100 Main Entry—Personal Name [mandatory if applicable]
110 Main Entry—Corporate Name [mandatory if applicable]
111 Main Entry—Meeting Name [mandatory if applicable]
130 Main Entry—Uniform Title [mandatory if applicable]

20X-24X Title and Title-Related Fields

240 Uniform Title [optional]
242 Translation of Title by Cataloging Agency [optional]
243 Collective Uniform Title [optional]
245 Title Statement [mandatory]

250-29X Edition, Imprint and Related Fields

250 Edition Statement [mandatory if applicable]
260 Publication, Distribution, Etc. (Imprint) [mandatory if applicable]

3XX Physical Description and Related Fields

300 Physical Description [mandatory]
340 Medium [mandatory if applicable]
351 Organization and Arrangement [optional]

4XX Series Statements

5XX Notes

500 General Note [optional]
502 Dissertation Note [optional]
505 Formatted Contents Note [optional]
 06 Restrictions on Access Note [optional]
510 Citation/References Note [optional]
518 Date and Place of Capture/Finding Note [optional]
520 Summary, Abstract, Annotation, Scope, etc. Note [optional]
521 Target Audience Note [optional]
524 Preferred Citation of Described Materials Note [optional]
530 Additional Physical Form Available Note [optional]
533 Reproduction Note [mandatory if applicable]
535 Location of Originals/Duplicates Note [optional]
540 Terms Governing Use and Reproduction Note [optional]
541 Immediate Source of Acquisition Note [optional]
544 Location of Associated Materials Note [optional]
545 Biographical or Historical Note [optional]
546 Language Note [optional]
555 Cumulative Index/Finding Aids Note [optional]
561 Provenance Note [optional]
562 Copy and Version Identification Note [optional]
565 Case File Characteristics Note [optional]
580 Linking Entry Complexity Note [mandatory if applicable]
581 Publications Note [optional]
583 Actions Note [optional]
584 Accumulation and Frequency of Use Note [optional]
59X Local Notes [optional]
* 590 Local Note [RLIN]

6XX Subject Access Fields

600 Subject Added Entry — Personal Name [mandatory if applicable]
610 Subject Added Entry — Corporate Name [mandatory if applicable]

611 Subject Added Entry—Meeting Name [mandatory if applicable]
630 Subject Added Entry—Uniform Title [mandatory if applicable]
650 Subject Added Entry—Topical Term [mandatory if applicable]
651 Subject Added Entry—Geographic Name [mandatory if applicable]
** 653 Index Term—Uncontrolled [validated for all formats except AMC]
655 Index Term—Genre/Form [optional]
656 Index Term—Occupation [optional]
657 Index Term—Function [optional]
69X Local Subject Access Fields [optional]
* 690 Local Subject Added Entry—Topical Term [RLIN]
* 691 Local Subject Added Entry—Geographic Name [RLIN]
* 696 Local Subject Added Entry—Personal Name [RLIN]
* 697 Local Subject Added Entry—Corporate Name [RLIN]
* 698 Local Subject Added Entry—Meeting Name [RLIN]
* 699 Local Subject Added Entry—Uniform Title [RLIN]

700-75X Added Entries

700 Added Entry—Personal Name [mandatory if applicable]
710 Added Entry—Corporate Name [mandatory if applicable]
711 Added Entry—Meeting Name [mandatory if applicable]
730 Added Entry—Uniform Title [mandatory if applicable]
740 Added Entry—Variant Title [mandatory if applicable]
752 Added Entry—Hierarchical Place Name [optional]
755 Added Entry—Physical Characteristics [optional]

76X-79X Linking Entries

773 Host Item Entry [mandatory if applicable]
* 789 Component Item Entry [RLIN]
* 796 Local Added Entry—Personal Name [RLIN]
* 797 Local Added Entry—Corporate Name [RLIN]
* 798 Local Added Entry—Meeting Name [RLIN]
* 799 Local Added Entry—Uniform Title [RLIN]

800-840 Series Added Entries

841-89X Holdings, Alternate Graphics, Etc.

851 Location [optional]
880 Alternate Graphic Representation [mandatory if applicable]
886 Foreign MARC Information Field [optional]

9XX Reserved for Local Implementation

* Defined by RLIN
** Will be validated for AMC with the implementation of format integration.

APPENDIX 2.

FULL SCHOLARLY DESCRIPTION OF HM 1035

[Reproduced by permission from Dutschke (1989), vol. 1, pp. 299-301.]

HM 1035   Southern Italy, s. XIII²
ARISTOTLE, DE ANIMALIBUS   *fig. 59*

ff. 1–98v: *Incipit liber primus aristotilis de naturis animalium quem transtulit magister michael scotus de greco in latinum et habet in se x libros. Rubrica,* Quedam partes corporum animalium dicuntur non composite et sunt partes que . . . attrahit partem spermatis et dimittit partem. [f. 46:] *Incipit liber primus de partibus animalium. In translatione vero nova,* In omni oppinione nobili et vili sunt duo modi dispositionum . . . per se et nos modo volumus incipere dicere de generatione animalium. [f. 69v, *De generatione animalium libri V:*] Etiam declaravi superius dispositionem membrorum animalium generaliter et specialiter . . . que accidunt non ex necessitate sed propter aliquid et propter causam finalem et propter causam moventem. Explicit liber aristotilis de naturis animalium. Sed intitulatus est et distinctus secundum novam translationem et sunt in hoc volumine 18 lib[ri, x] de hystoriis animalium, 3 de partibus animalium et v de generatione animalium, vii^us de progressu animalium hic deficit cum quo essent xix.

Aristotle, *De naturis animalium, De partibus animalium, De generatione animalium,* trans. Michael Scot, completed by 1220; text not printed in full. See *AL* 80–81 and 245 where this manuscript is described. The text here is complete: the scribe erroneously repeated the rubric of Book VII on f. 26, thus his calculations at the end of the manuscript were off by one. Marginalia and nota marks by various readers of the fourteenth and fifteenth centuries.

Parchment (prepared in the Italian manner), ff. i (early modern paper) + 98 + i (early modern paper); 368 × 240 (237 × 140) mm. 1–8¹² 9². Catchwords in inner right corner, decorated with 4 pattes-de-mouche; leaves signed in roman numerals, except on quire 8 where they are signed a–f. 2 columns of 52 lines, ruled in lead with single bounding lines and a set of double outer rules in all 4 margins; pricking for the various frame rules visible in all 4 margins (none noticed for the line rules). Written in a minuscule book hand.

Opening historiated initial, 8-line, in dull pink set on a gold ground, depicting a cleric showing a group of animals to monks and students; C-shaped border in dull pink, blue, green, ochre and orange with biting animal heads and vines as pinwheels sprouting rounded trilobe leaves, the points of which often terminate in gold dots, in a style somewhat similar to A. Daneu Lattanzi, *Lineamenti di Storia della Miniatura in Sicilia* (Florence 1966) fig. 43 and 44 of Vatican Library, Vat. lat. 36; 3 coats of arms in roundels in the lower border: 2 erased; one remains (see below). Major initials for the divisions of Books, 9- to 6-line (e.g. ff. 5v, 8, 9), parted red and blue with filigree and tendrils in both colors; secondary initials, 3- or 2-line, in alternating red or blue with flourishing of the other color; alternating red and blue paragraph marks and letters of the running headlines. Rubrics present for the Books only up to f. 46; thereafter both Book and chapter headings noted in the margins in a fifteenth century cursive hand. Fifteenth century foliation, 131–229; on f. 98v (i.e. 229v), in a fifteenth century hand, "sono carte cc xxx."

Bound, s. XVI (?), in limp parchment with title on the spine in a decorative gothic hand, but considerably damaged: "509. Arist. L[ogi?]ca Decor⟨?⟩ ⟨?⟩oli⟨?⟩ ⟨?⟩s de animali-[bus] Manuscript"; fore edge ties missing. On the back flyleaf, offset of a strip print [Woodward del. Rowlandson f.] *Borders for Rooms,* Plate 2, London, March 25 1799 at Ackerman's Gallery, 101 Strand.

Written in southern Italy for a member of the family of Charles I of Anjou, King of Sicily and Naples, 1266–85; the remaining coat of arms on f. 1 is of Anjou: azure, semy of fleur-de-lys or, differenced with a label of 5 points gules (Rietstap, vol. 1, pl. 52); Mr. Van de Put, according to De Ricci, has suggested that the 2 erased coats of arms are Jerusalem (Charles I was crowned King of Jerusalem in 1278) and Hungary ancient (Charles II married Mary of Hungary in 1270); both erased coats of arms bear traces of tinctures in gules and or. Belonged to Pier Leoni (d. 1492), physician to Lorenzo de' Medici. The inventory of Leoni's books is published in L. Dorez, "Recherches sur la bibliothèque de Pier Leoni, médecin de Laurent de Médicis," *Revue des Bibliothèques* 7 (1897) 81–106, where this manuscript may be identified with item 8, "Aristoteles de natura animalium." The single title, corresponding to HM 1035 as it stands today, suggests that the book had been bound in its more complete state (cf. the multiple titles on the spine, which must have referred to the text[s] on the missing 130 folios at the beginning of the book) and had then been dismembered before 1582, when the inventory of Leoni's library was compiled. See J. Ruysschaert, "Nouvelles recherches au sujet de la bibliothèque de Pier Leoni, médecin de Laurent le Magnifique," *Bulletin de la classe des lettres et des sciences morales et politiques de l'Académie royale de Belgique,* ser. 5, 46 (1960) 37–

65, and his introduction to *Bibliothecae Apostolicae Vaticanae . . . Codices 11414–11709* (Vatican 1959) p. vii, mentioning HM 1034 (evidently as typographical error for HM 1035): a number of Leoni books were in the library of the Jesuit College in Rome until ca. 1912, when approximately 27 of their manuscripts were sold to the bookdealer W. Voynich, possibly including HM 1035. On the front pastedown in modern pencil: J991, J992; on f. 1, in modern pencil: 992, a8665a. Acquired by Henry E. Huntington in 1918 from G. D. Smith.

Secundo folio: et pulcro sono
Bibliography: De Ricci, 82. *Aspects of Medieval England*, n. 41 open at f. 1.

APPENDIX 3.

TAGGED MARC RECORD
FOR HUNTINGTON LIBRARY, HM 1035

[Fixed field omitted; 0XX control fields omitted]

100 00	Aristotle.
245 00	Incipit liber primus aristotilis de naturis animalium quem transtulit magister michaelis scotus de greco in latinum et habet in se x libros.
260	$c [1251-1300]
300	98 leaves (2 columns, 52 lines), bound: $b parchment; $c 37 cm.
500	Caption title from f. 1r.
500	Translated from the Arabic before 1220.
500	Includes: Historia animalium (ff. 1r-46r) — De partibus animalium (ff. 46r-69v) — De generatione animalium (ff. 69v-98v).
500	Written in a minuscule book hand.
500	Historiated initial on gold ground and colored border on f. 1r; 9-6 line initials for divisions of books and 3-2 line minor initials in red and blue, with red and blue flourishing; paragraph marks and letters of the running headlines in alternating red and blue.
500	Collation: 1-8^{12} 9^2.
500	Catchwords in inner right corner; leaves signed in roman numerals; ruled in lead; prickings for the frame rules only visible in all four margins.
500	Fifteenth-century foliation 131-229.

500	Marginalia and nota marks by various readers of the 14th and 15th centuries; booksellers' codes in modern pencil on front pastedown and f. 1r.
500	Bound in limp parchment, probably 16th cent.
561	Written in southern Italy for a member of the family of Charles I of Anjou, King of Sicily and Naples, 1266-85; the arms of Anjou on f. 1r, with two erased coats of arms, probably Jerusalem and Hungary.
561	Belonged to Pier Leoni, physician to Lorenzo de' Medici; later to the Jesuit college at Rome; possibly sold to W. Voynich ca. 1912.
541	Acquired from G.D. Smith by Henry E. Huntington in 1918.
510 4	Aristoteles latinus, $c I, p. 80-81, 245
510 4	Ricci, $c p. 82
510 4	Aspects of Medieval England, $c 41
555 8	Described in: Guide to Medieval and Renaissance Manuscripts in the Huntington Library (Huntington Library, 1989).
524	Huntington Library, HM 1035.
506	Access restricted.
650 10	Animals.
650 10	Zoology $x Pre-Linnean works.
700 10	Aristotle. $t De naturis animalium.
700 02	Aristotle. $t Historia animalium.
700 02	Aristotle. $t De partibus animalium.
700 02	Aristotle. $t De generatione animalium.
700 11	Scot, Michael, $e trans.
700 01	Charles, $b I, $c King of Anjou, $e associated name.
700 11	Leoni, Pier, $e former owner.
710 21	Jesuit College at Rome, $e former owner.
700 11	Voynich, W., $e former owner.
700 11	Smith, G. D., $e former owner.
755	Limp bindings. $2rbbin
755	Vellum bindings. $2rbbin
755	Markings. $2rbprov
755	Codes. $2rbprov

APPENDIX 4.

FORMATTED MARC RECORD
FOR HUNTINGTON LIBRARY, HM 1035

Aristotle.

Incipit liber primus aristotilis de naturis animalium quem transtulit magister michaelis scotus de greco in latinum et habet in se x libros. − [1251-1300]

98 leaves (2 columns, 52 lines), bound: parchment; 37 cm.

Caption title from f. 1r.

Translated from the Arabic before 1220.

Includes: Historia animalium (ff. 1r-46r); De partibus animalium (ff. 46r-69v); De generatione animalium (ff. 69v-98v).

Written in a minuscule book hand.

Historiated initial on gold ground and colored border on f. 1r; 9-6 line initials for divisions of books and 3-2 line minor initials in red and blue, with red and blue flourishing; paragraph marks and letters of the running headlines in alternating red and blue.

Collation: 1-8^{12} 9^2.

Catchwords in inner right corner; leaves signed in roman numerals; ruled in lead; prickings for the frame rules only visible in all four margins.

Fifteenth-century foliation 131-229.

Marginalia and nota marks by various readers of the 14th and 15th centuries; booksellers' codes in modern pencil on front pastedown and f. 1r.

Bound in limp parchment, probably 16th cent.

Written in southern Italy for a member of the family of Charles I of Anjou, King of Sicily and Naples, 1266-85; the arms of Anjou on f. 1r, with two erased coats of arms, probably Jerusalem and Hungary.

Belonged to Pier Leoni, physician to Lorenzo de' Medici; later to the Jesuit college at Rome; possibly sold to W. Voynich ca. 1912.

Acquired from G.D. Smith by Henry E. Huntington in 1918.

References: Aristoteles latinus, I, p. 245; Ricci, p. 82; Aspects of Medieval England, 41.

Described in: Guide to Medieval and Renaissance Manuscripts in
   the Huntington Library (Huntington Library, 1989).
Cite as: Huntington Library, HM 1035.
Access restricted.

SUBJECTS: 1.__Animals. 2.__Zoology — Pre-Linean works.

NAMES AND TITLES: 1. Aristotle. De naturis animalium.
   2. Aristotle. Historia animalium. 3. Aristotle. De partibus animalium. 4. Aristotle. De generatione animalium. 5. Scot, Michael,
   trans. 6. Charles, I, King of Anjou, associated name. 7. Leoni,
   Pier, former owner. 8. Jesuit College at Rome, former owner.
   9. Voynich, W., former owner. 10. Smith, G. D., former owner.

PHYSICAL CHARACTERISTICS: 1. Limp bindings. 2. Vellum
   bindings. 3. Markings. 4. Codes.

[INDEXES NEEDED: Place of origin; Date; Repository; Physical
   characteristics of medieval codices]

APPENDIX 5.

FULL SCHOLARLY DESCRIPTION
OF HM 64

[Reproduced by permission from Dutschke (1989), vol. 1, pp. 130-139.]

HM 64   England, s. XV^ex

ASTROLOGICAL and MEDICAL COMPILATION

1. f. 1r–v: [Explanations of the tables on ff. 2–17] *Ad noticiam istius kalendarii habendam,* Est notandum quod in prima linea descendendo versus sinistram scribitur numerus dierum . . . [art. 2]; Sequitur kalendarium Commune [art. 2]. Postea annectuntur tria tria [*sic*] cicli coniunccionum et apposicionum verarum Solis et lune . . . [art. 2]; Deinde sequitur tabula docens quis sit Annus Bisextilis que littera dominicalis que indiccio et que primacio lune . . . [art. 3]; Post hec sequitur tabula festorum mobilium . . . [art 3]; Item sequitur tabula planetarum docens quis planeta regnat qualibet hora artificiali . . . [art. 4]; Secuntur homo venarum et tabula lune cum canonibus [arts. 5–6]. Item sequitur tabula Eclipsium solis et Lune . . . [art. 7]; Sequitur homo Signorum cum Canone [arts. 8–9]. Secuntur spera Pictagoris cum canone et sic ultra et cetera [art. 12].

2. ff. 2–7v: Full calendar in red and black, not graded, with extensive computistic columns in cycles from 1480 to 1520; among the feasts are "Prima pascha" (22 March, in red); "Adam creatus est" (23 March, in red), "Resurrectio domini" (27 March, in red); Richard of Chichester (3 April), "Egressio noie de Archa" (26 April, in red); Translation of Elizabeth of Hungary (2 May), Translation of Richard of Chichester (16 June), Etheldreda (23 June), Visitation (2 July, in red), Translation of Osmund (16 July), Transfiguration (7 August, in red), Gabriel archangel and Antoninus of Palencia (2 September), Modwenna (9 September), Translation of Etheldreda (17 October), Frideswide (19 October), Elizabeth of Hungary (19 November), Osmund (4 December); Latin month verses: Principium iani sancit tropicus capricorni (Walther, *Initia* 14721); Prima dies mensis et septima truncat ut ensis (Walther, *Initia* 14563).

3. f. 8: Tables of indictions, beginning in 1460, and of movable feasts.

4. f. 8v: Table of ascendancy of planets.

5. ff. 8v–10v: Vein Man: f. 9, *Ad minuendum sanguinem,* At the auctoritate of Ipocras the Nobell phesiscion Isodore tellithe that there beþe thre dayes in the yere in the whiche men schulde not blede . . . The 2 vaynes in þe Corners of þe eyen nexte þe nose seruen for derkenys of the eyen webbes clowtis & pynes of þe eyen & all fluxis & erenaundes of þe eyen et cetera. *Explicit tabula venarum.*

6. ff. 10v–11: *Canon Signorum,* Tabula lune ad sciendum eius Signum et gradum omni die in quo luna est . . . Et quia Aries in prima mundi constitucionem cepit vergi inde est quod caput hominis habere dicitur . . . [with table of reigning zodiac sign for each month and table of solar and lunar degrees].

7. ff. 11v–12: Pages ruled, but blank, for tables of eclipses; f. 12, Hit is to vnderstonde that in the Eclipsis of the Sonn and the mone is to knowe wahat party of the body schalbe derke . . . [with diagram labelled *Figura Eclipsis*].

8. f. 12v: *Homo signorum, Aries,* Cave ab inscicione a luna existente in Ariete, caveas medicari in capite . . . [with Zodiac Man]; *Contra vermes,* Qui super se istos 2os versus portaverit omnes vermes interficerit. Dum appropriant super me nocentes ut edant carnes meas . . . ; Beatus Iob vermes huic et sicut deo placuit . . .

9. f. 13: Table to determine when the sun enters a sign of the zodiac, with columns for the sign, month, day, hour, minute, planet, and part of the body affected (this last given in French).

10. ff. 13v–14: *Ignea:* Signum mobile, Aries; Signum fixum, Leo; Signum commune, Sagittarius. Ista sunt signa diei Masculini . . . [table of relationships between the 4 elements and the 12 signs of the zodiac]; Biware howe thou the body keytte/ For the blode may not to faste out fleitte . . . [Schuler, n. 60; Hanna, "Addenda," n. 6]; f. 14, Zodiac Man, marked for bloodletting under specific planets.

11. f. 14v: *Ad sciendum gradus siccitatis et Caliditatis,* Primus gradus Caliditatis est cum aliqua res habeant unam porcionem frigiditatis . . . ; *De etate Lune quando est Sicca vel calida,* Prima etas lune est et humida Calida . . . ; *Satera* is a thyng that bygynnythe goodely and so endithe. *Commeda* is he that begynnythe laborusly . . . *Tregedia* is he that begynnythe ioyfully . . . *Demagogus* is he that folowithe his owne will . . . ; *De signis mobilibus et fixis et eorum condicionibus,* In signis fixis debet incipi opus quod multum dare debet ut edificia . . .

12. ff. 14v–16v: *Hic incipit Canon et Figura Spere,* Spera Apulagii et platonis de vita et morte et de omnibus rebus negociis que inquirere volueris quis Primo computa per omnes litteras ut puta de nomine egrum, addes lunam quota fuerit diei quo inciderit Eger . . . ; [f. 15v:] This is the spere of Pictogoras that appolyn drewe by the whyche a man may wite and knowe what thyng that he will as of a Sike man or woman or childe . . . [with diagrams of the spheres of Pythagoras and Apuleius Platonicus to prognosticate life, death, victory, safe return from a journey, etc. according to the number of letters in the individual's name in varying calculations]; f. 16v, *Experimenta de vita et de morte,* Pone desuper urinam infirmi lac mulieris que peperit masculum . . . [5 such tests]; *Signa mortifera,* Quando frons rubit supercylya declinantur . . . ; *Galienus Signa mortis,* Frons erit plana sine rugis . . . ; *Nota versus de signis mortalibus,* Hiis signis moriens tactis dinoscitur eger/ Fronte rubet primo pedibus frigescit ab ymo . . . [Walther, *Initia* 8211]; *Qui bene degerit non ingerit est homo sanus; De signis mortalibus in acutis febribus si de vita vel de morte* Egrotantis in acutis febribus Scire volueris . . .

13. ff. 16v–17: *Ad cognossendum pulsum Alicuius,* To knowe the pulsse Laye thy 4 fyngers and towche the pulsse . . . and so goynge Adowneward betokeny-the dethe et cetera.

14. f. 17: T-O world map; diagram of the universe in concentric circles from hell to the "Sedes dei"; diagrams of solar and lunar eclipses.

15. f. 17v: Ad habendum in quo signo et in qua mansione fuerit luna singulis horis insume lunam . . . In two dayes 6 howris & 40 minutes the mone gothe thorowe a signe . . . as the Sonne dothe in 30 dayes.

Excerpts largely from the Ps. Aristotelian *Secreta secretorum;* Thorndike and Kibre, 42 (?).

16. ff. 17v, 21v, 34, 51: Charms numbered 1–5, consisting of variously formed crosses within inscribed circles: f. 17v, *Contra inimicus* [*sic*], *1,* Si quis hoc signum super se portat nequid capi ab Inimicus [*sic*]; f. 21v, *Contra mortem subitam, 2,* Qui hoc signum super se portat sine confessione non morietur; f. 34, *Pro victoria, 3,* Hoc signum misit deus Regi Tedeon [?] qui cum isto pugnat victoriam habebit; f. 34, *Pro Igni, 4,* Hoc signum crucis portans se non timebis ignem, [below the circle:] In quacumque domo ubi [the charm] fecerit vel ymago Virginis Dorothee eximie matris [*sic*] alme, Nullus abortivus infantis nascetur in illa . . . ; f. 51, *Contra Demones, 5,* Signum sancti Michaelis quas omnes demones timent die qua videris demones non timebis. [blank circle, with band for inscription of a similar charm (?) on f. 1v].

17. ff. 18–21v: *Galieni Medici Regimen Sanitatis feliciter incipit,* In hoc tractatu et qui intitulantur [*sic*] de Regimine Sanitatis aliquid Breviter dicendum est cum christo adiutorio de aliquibus . . . [Text:] *De utilitate boni regiminis,* Oportet illum qui wlt esse longevus . . . unde de talibus potest dici quod si non desistant percuscionem non evadent. *Explicit tractatus compendiosus de regimine Sanitatis.* [followed by charm; see art. 16].

Thorndike and Kibre, 1011 and 1614 as Bartholomeus de Ferraria.

18. ff. 22–25v: Approximately 40 medical recipes or dietary recommendations in English, including one in verse (f. 22v), *A diet for man that is brusid or bete,* Whoso be woundid or evill Beete/ Garlike ne oynonys maye he non ete . . . [Schuler, n. 280; Hanna, "Addenda," n. 65]; an incantation to staunch blood (f. 23), Longinus miles latus domini nostri ihesu cristi lancia perforavit . . . Cristus et Iohannes descenderunt in flumine Iordani . . . ; 7 recipes for pigments.

19. ff. 26–28v: *In nomine sancte individue Trinitatis et* gloriose virginis marie et ad utilitatem hominum et personarum confortacionem lapsorumque reformacionem. Volo aliqua de pestilencia scribere ex dictis Auctorum magis Autenticorum breviter compilenda quia pestilencia nos invadit plus quam manserat ipsos antiquos . . . Si autem transit ad fundum urine insequente ebdomada vel in alia sequenti·veraciter morietur et hoc est verum. Et hec de pestilentia. Et deus adiuvet nos omnes de tali morbo. Amen.

Excerpts largely from the work of Johannes Jacobi; cf. edition by K. Sudhoff, "Pestschriften aus den ersten 150 Jahren nach der Epidemie des 'schwarzen Todes' 1348," *Archiv für Geschichte der Medizin* 17 (1925) 16–32; Thorndike and Kibre, 698 (?) and 1709.

20. ff. 28v–34: *Hic incipit Trotula minor de ornatu. De fessurus* [sic] *labiorum,* Sunt quidem qui fissuras labiorum paciuntur . . . ungatur oculos cum custodiat et mane lavet cum aqua Tepida. *Explicit Trotula.* [followed by charms; see art. 16].

Portions of 2 treatises commonly called *Trotula minor:* 33 chapters from the end of *Ut de curis mulierum* (interrupted by the loss of a leaf in the chapter "De Sorditate aurium") followed by (ff. 30–34) a nearly full text of *De ornatu,* beginning Ut mulier suavissima et planissima. . . ; Thorndike and Kibre, 284, 1612.

21. ff. 34v–38v: Medical recommendations mainly in Latin, both in verse and in prose; f. 34v, verses on factors in prescribing medicines (Walther, *Initia* 17786), on the 4 humors, on medicines applied externally, on dangers to health, a prose passage on the combination of medicines with the appropriate time of day and year; f. 35, 2 recipes (of which one in French), verses on a short and happy life, prose and verses on considerations necessary for diagnosis, 4 sets of verses on good health (of which one Walther, *Initia* 18083); f. 35v, notes on various medical matters, verses on pleurisy, on pulse, notes on various medical matters entitled *Verba constantine;* ff. 35v–38v, verses, mainly dietary, written without break, with rubrics such as *herbe pro potu, locio manus, De pane, De carnibus porcinis, Potus et prandio, Ova, Raphanus, Porrus, Piper, Crocus, Faba, Lac, Butirum, Ficus, Cervisia, Pomum granatum, Siler, Feniculis:* Salgia cum ruta facient tua pocula tuta/ Adde rose florem minunt potenter Amorem . . . Cum carni carwey non sine febre fui et cetera; f. 38v, *Salve stella maris mater dei vite* (with the vowels numbered, "a" as 1, "e" as 2, "i" as 3).

22. ff. 38v–50: Omnis urina est Colamentum Sa[n]guinis et est duarum rerum proprie Significativa . . . [Text:] In the begynynge thou schalt take hede to fowre thyngis that longithe to the dome of vryne . . . The 37[th] vrine Red as Bloode ouer all signifiethe menys strene et cetera.

Thorndike and Kibre, 1004, here missing one leaf after f. 38 with loss of text; illustrated with drawings of urine bottles, not colored in.

23. ff. 50–51: *Here Bygynnythe the Tokenys that Ipocrace the goode leche wrote for to knowe the sike if he myght be helid By medycyn or noo and here bygynnythe the Tokenys Furste at the hedde and othere Tokenys folluynge et cetera,* Whoso of dolowre or ache in the hedde have or swellynge in the face withe owte redde at the leste . . . or lesses his clothis a man that is frangticke hit be Tokenys that he schall dye on the same evill et cetera. *Explicit.* [followed by charm; see art. 16].

24. f. 51r–v: *For to make a white Entret,* Whoso will a white Entrete make/ Wirgyn waxe & honny he muste take . . . [Schuler, n. 600; Hanna, "Addenda," n. 70]; 10 other recipes in English and in Latin, including indices of pregnancy and of the sex of the fetus.

25. ff. 52–61v: Here Begynnes the Booke of Astronomye and of philosofye contryuyd and made of þe wisseste Philosophers and Astronemers that euer were . . . he schall leve longe but if the Cours of the mone be contraye [sic] to hym et cetera.

A shorter version of this text in J. Krochalis and E. Peters, eds., *The World of Piers Plowman* (University of Pennsylvania Press 1975) 5–17.

26. ff. 61v–62: *This is the Booke that Ipocrace made to the kynge of all Bestis alyve to knowe,* And this booke he sayde and sende to the Emperowre of Constantyne the Nowbull the whiche booke is full of trewe mediacions & medicynys prouyd to all the memberis of manys body that is made of 4 humerus . . . and yenste flewmatike that is colde and moyste Ye schall geve therayenste hoote and Dye [*sic*].

Text on the 4 humors; see R. H. Robbins, "Medical Manuscripts in Middle English," *Speculum* 45 (1970) 409, n. 47.

27. ff. 62–63: Hit to be knowen well that purgacions & laxatiffes in somer sesson lightly engenderiþe ebullicions and swellyngis of the longus . . . and hit schall gon owte thorowe castynge agaynes Appetit and the affectis schall Ben lessid.

Text on prescription of laxatives at different times of the year.

28. ff. 63–72: *Here begynnys the Booke of Destenarye of the 12 Signes by there Cours as they Raynes in the yere Sol in Ariete,* Nowe hit is to declare and Determe of the 12 signys and of there kyndis what euery is ordyned to be by the waye of kynde and predistinacion . . . And his evill dayes bethe Mars and Saturnus And if ye vill skape from thes forsayde poyntis doo as hit is byforesayde.

Text on male and female complexions as determined by birth dates and influence of the zodiac; often continuous with the text of art. 25.

29. f. 72: Notes on the use of arabic and roman numerals and a brief chronology *Ab origine mundi* to *Anno Regni Regis Henri 7° post conquestum.*

30. ff. 72v–79: The right Pitte of helle is amydys the erthe withein/ Owre lorde that all made I wisse quenyte was of syn . . . Now godde that vs sowle gave vs lete hire here so rede/ That saynte mychall hit mote amonge & byfore hym leede.

IMEV 3453.

31. f. 79: Septem sunt planete secundum dicta philosophorum silicet Saturnus . . . et quolibet Miliare sit Duorum Millium passum et cetera [note on measuring distances between the planets]; recipe in English.

32. ff. 79v–81: *Here saythe Galianus the goode Leche that was of metis and dryngkis to vse in tyme of the yere in every monythe to take and Ete & in tyme of Bloode Letynge et cetera. Aquarius,* In the monythe of Ianyver whyte wynes dryngke & Blode letynge forbeere . . . and a grete pestelence ouer all placis Si luna fuerit in capricornio ad propositum tuum ire noli. *This ben the tokones that schall fall of all the Mistis and the Thonderynge & when to take yowre Iournaye . . .*

G. Henslow, *Medical Works of the Fourteenth Century* (London 1899) 62–65.

33. f. 81: Seven medical recipes in English.

34. ff. 81v–83: *Now hit is to knowe that what Man that will well and parffitly deme the levynge and predistynacion of man or woman by this foresayde Signes 12 and 7 planettes and 4 Elymentis . . . ,* Also there bethe 3 parellus mundayes in the yere that won is the furste mondaye of Feverell . . . And the laste daye

of Feuerree no man schulde Blede for hit is forboden of olde tyme as thes wyse masteris yete wittenys et cetera.

Text on perilous days, in particular for birth of children, eating goose and bloodletting.

35. f. 83: Six medical recipes in English.

36. ff. 83v–93v: [*Storia Lune*] Gode that all this worlde wroughte/ And all mankynde withe his blode bowghte . . . [f. 84, Text:] *Luna prima Bonum*, The furste daye of the mon/ God wiste full well what was to done . . . [f. 93:] But what childe that daye Iboore Is/ Hit schall be goode bothe ware and wisse/ *Nota*, Nowe have ye herde all this storye/ Every crature to rewell hym bye . . . To send vs happe and grace/ And hye in heveyn to have a place. Amen. *IMEV 970.*

37. f. 93v: Four medical recipes in English.

38. ff. 94–95: [Calendarial prognostics] Listenythe now & ye schall hyre/ Talkynge of a goode matere . . . [Text:] *Littera Dominicalis*, Ba comyn wynter a wete somer/ Dirthe of corne lightenynge & thonder . . . Grawnt vs all thy dire blessynge/· That we maye com to thy blysse euerlastynge. *Explicit.* *IMEV 1905.*

39. f. 95: Two medical recipes in English.

40. ff. 95v–101: *Tractatus mirabilis aquarum* Quas composuit Petrus Hispanensis cum Naturali industria quarum prima est herba et est mirabilis in virtute ad visum clarificandum . . . , Accipe rute finiculi . . . [*Aqua Silicis hoc modo debet fieri* . . .] et fac ignem fortem de carbonibus et erit quod vis.

Thorndike and Kibre, 1328 (?), with some recipes in English (mainly for *aqua vite* on ff. 96v–99), and others in Latin including one for making and extinguishing Greek fire (f. 100r–v) and several for dying cloth (f. 101); the distinction between this and the following article is unclear.

41. ff. 101v–103: Approximately 20 recipes including one in French (f. 101v), *Pur le medicine du solaile*; one for an oil to color gold, tin and copper and one to color lead (these 2 crossed out); one to make worms; one in English to gild silver (ff. 101v–102); an incantation (f. 102v) to staunch blood, Ihesus criste that was borne in Bethelem . . . Ihesus criste that was baptissed in the water of flumeiourdan withstonde this blode . . . *Item ad Sanguinem Restituendum*, In nomine patris . . . Ego coniuro te Sanguis ad Restituendum per patrem . . . ; a recipe in English (f. 102v), "for to make won to seme am3sell [in cipher]"; one in English to write on a knife; one in English to write on a sword (ff. 102v–103).

42. ff. 103–104: *Here bygynnys the makynge of the 9 marvelous waters the whiche Peter of Spayne made and founde hem by his owne kyndely witte of the whiche the Furst is clepid the precious water of herbis* . . . *Item pro oculis bona aqua que vocatur lumen oculorum*, Take rewe fenell . . . for hit Brennythe as ewe ardent as moche for to saye as water Brenynge and hit is goode for the colde gowte.

An English translation of a portion of Petrus Hispanus, *Liber de oculo*, of which the Latin is above, f. 95v; the text here diverges from the Latin after the fifth water and continues without break (art. 43).

43. ff. 104–113: Approximately 140 recipes, mainly in English, including several to dye cloth (ff. 107–108), one for palsy proved by "Master Swan," an incantation to staunch blood, As wisshly as a prestis woman schall be the devillis roode horsse or beste so wisshely staunche the Bloode of this man . . . , a passage on the magical and medical *virtutes de Betonice* (ff. 108v–109), several incantations to cure epilepsy (ff. 110v–111), an incantation to staunch blood, Longeus [*sic*] miles ebreus Latus domini nostri ihesu christi lancea perforavit . . . Et sicut restitit aquam Iourdanus in qua Baptizatus est christus . . . (f. 111v), and one for a quick delivery, beginning with the word square, Sator arepo tenet opera rotas (Walther, *Initia* 17297).

44. ff. 113v–120: *Here bygynnys a boke of many medycins for many evilles that spryngithe in mankynde The whiche medicyns the wyse leche Galian & aschofus and Ipocras made in here tyme . . . & for eysy vnderstondynge here have I drawe hem oute of dyuers longage in to englisshe tonge.* Hic incipit medicine optime probate, In 4 partes of euery man/ Bygynnes the sickenys that ye han/ In hedde in wombe or in the Splene/ Or in the bladder the 4 l mene . . . & put hit in to a Boxe withe that anoynte the hedde till be hoole for this is provid sikurlye.

IMEV 1408, Schuler, n. 191, 292, 518 and Hanna, "Addenda," n. 21; here (and below, ff. 145v–147) written in prose form and incorporating approximately 65 prose recipes in English including 2 *Gracia dei* ointments (f. 117r–v), one of "the Ladi Beawschampe the Erllis Wiffe of Warwike" and the other "that the Erle of harfforde wssid that was holden a nowbull Surgeon"; on f. 118, indices for determining if a sick person will live or die.

45. f. 120: Hec sunt semina 4^{or} frigidorum maiorum scilicet Semen Cucurbite, Semen Ciculi . . . ; recipe in Latin.

46. ff. 120–121v: Approximately 55 gynecological recipes in Latin, citing an authority for each (Galen, Isaac Judaeus, Dioscorides, Macer, Petrus Lucrator, *Lapidarius*, Hippocrates, Constantinus).

47. f. 121v: Libra continet 12 uncias et ista figura ʒ significat unciam. Uncia continet Octo dragmas . . . [note on pharmaceutical weights].

48. ff. 121v–124v: *Hic incipit secundus liber*, Si collum wlneratur cum ense vel autem telo sibi primo perfecte videat et sciat digito si os . . .
Pharmaceutical recipes and surgical procedures for wounds, abscesses, cankers, leprosy, dislocated jaws, hernias, cataracts, etc.

49. ff. 125–135: *Hic incipit quid pro quo*, Quoniam autem ea que sunt utilia in curationibus inveniri quandoque non possunt dicamus quid pro quo debet poni. Absinthium gallice Aloyne anglice wermode, calidum in 1° et siccum in 2° grado. Absinthium ponticum, centonica, sewermode . . . Zedorarium, Red woll, circa instans. Zuctara, circa instans. [below an empty space, at the end of the column:] Pro vino malorum granatorum potest poni succus. Accede ut

dicunt [?] magister poncius vel magister henricus. De carnoco qui scripsit istud quid pro quo, deo gracias et cetera.

Thorndike and Kibre, 206, 295, 325, 1274, 1295.

50. ff. 135v–138: Approximately 25 passages in Latin, some recipes, the others descriptions of sicknesses, such as *Herniafrondisia, Species autem hernie, Capitulum de lapide qui nascitur in vesica, De cura lapidis per incisionem, De cura lapidis Mulierum;* an incantation to protect one's sheep (ff. 137v–138), a prayer for those who are loosing blood, a charm to staunch blood by writing across the patient's forehead with his own blood, *Sessa sonus Sonus sessa Beronis beronissa.*

51. ff. 138–143: Approximately 60 recipes in English including charms to cure dog bite, to dissolve spots in one's eyes, for a speedy delivery; a long incantation of "Saynte Susan" to the Five Wounds of Christ to heal a wound (printed by F. Heinrich, ed., *Ein mittelenglische Medizinbuch,* Halle, 1895, pp. 163–66), 3 charms for fevers (the last, of Peter outside the Latin Gate), a charm against worms (these 5 charms, ff. 140–141v, lined through); indices to determine if a woman is a virgin or not (f. 141v) and to determine who is at fault if a couple has no children (f. 142v).

52. f. 143r–v: *Hic incipit tractatus de virtutibus corei serpentis secundum Iohannem pallium,* De combustione vel pulverisacione Corei serpentis habet pulverisari isto modo, fac ignem magnam ex carbonibus . . . To knowe the vertues of an Adders skynne. When Ihon & powle were in þe Cite of Alexandre there they founde a booke the whiche was callid Salus vite. In this Booke was wreten 12 Experimentis of the Adders skynne . . . & more prophete to manys Boodye then this is probatum est.

J. W. S. Johnson, "Les 'Experimenta duodecim Johannis Paulini,' " *Bulletin de la Société française d'historie de la médecine* 12 (1913) 257–68, for another version. Thorndike and Kibre, 295, 525, 782.

53. ff. 143v–176: Approximately 450 medical recipes, mainly in English, including many charms, frequently lined through: ff. 144v–145, a charm in French and Latin to heal a wound by placing over it a plate of lead bearing Maltese crosses in the 4 corners and a fifth in the center (diagram, f. 145); f. 145, 2 charms in English verse, the first for limbs "that ar myswreyght," Oure lorde Ihesu Criste/ ouere a den roode/ And his foole sloode . . . [Schuler, n. 412; Hanna, "Addenda," n. 42] and the second for toothache, Byfore the gate of Galile/ Saynte Petur ther sate hee . . . [Hanna, "Addenda," n. 5]; ff. 145v–147, portions of *IMEV* 1408 [Schuler, n. 206, 208, 226, 514, 516; Hanna, "Addenda," n. 21; art. 44 above]; f. 149r–v, 2 cosmetics for a "fayre face"; f. 149v, means to prevent drunkenness, in Latin; f. 149v, a charm against toothache, in Latin; f. 158, a recipe for toothpaste; f. 158, a charm to staunch blood, Ihesus that was in Bethelem Borne and Baptised in flome Iourdane . . . ; f. 162r–v, a charm to staunch blood, Stabat ihesus contra flumen iordanis . . . Longinus miles latus domini nostri ihesu christi lancea perforavit . . . ; ff. 162v–163, 2 charms, one in Latin "for woundes withe oyle and wolle" and the second in English verse, I coniure the wonde blyve/ by the vertu of the woundes fyve . . . [Schuler, n. 288; Hanna, "Addenda," n. 16]; f. 163, a charm to be worn

for protection against evil spirits; f. 163r–v, a charm for a speedy childbirth with the usual word square, Sator arepo . . . ; f. 168, 2 charms against fevers, the first to be written on 3 apples or "oblata" and the second to be written on 3 sage leaves and given to the patient to eat on successive days; f. 170, a charm against moles.

54. ff. 176v–183v: *Asterion* Is an herbe that men clepithe Lunare. This herbe growithe amongis stonys and in hye placis . . . [*Quinque folium* . . . :] Also for Brenynge of Lemes take the Iuce and dryngke hit and ye schall be hoole et cetera. *Explecet*.

G. Brodin, ed., *Agnus Castus: a Middle English Herbal*. Essays and Studies on English Language and Literature 6 (Copenhagen and Cambridge, Mass., 1950), this manuscript unrecorded; text has 79 entries, largely in the order of the printed edition, but omitting many of them and ending incomplete at *Quinque folium*.

55. ff. 184–190v: Aloes lignum, sunt autem tria Genera Ligni. Aloes est enim que Reperitur in insula que dicitur Cume . . . . Salix arbor est gallice Saus. Saturea id est ysopus agresta.

Glossary of herbs in Latin with some English and French equivalents. J. Stannard, "A Fifteenth Century Botanical Glossary," *Isis* 55 (1964) 353–67.

56. ff. 191–196v: *Hic incipiunt experimenta secreta et experta. Nota de urinis et pro dolore capitis,* Item est intelligendum quod si urina mingitur turbulenta et sic maneat, tunc significat dolorem capitis presentem . . . *Contra litargiam,* Tota pellis leporis cum Auribus et unguibus combusta est [catchword:] pulvis//

Approximately 180 recipes in Latin, from the head downwards, then beginning again on f. 196 with the head (and the related sicknesses: frensy, epilepsy and lethargy), ending defectively; material includes a charm against headache (f. 191r–v), 2 charms against nosebleed (f. 192), the first suspending herbs from the patient's neck and the second by writing on his forehead, a charm against toothache by writing on the patient's jaw, and a recipe in French (f. 196).

57. ff. 176, 183v, 184v, 186, 186v, 187 (an ointment "quod Iohn harris pottycary"), 188v, 190: 18 medical recipes in English, added s. XV and XVI.

Paper, untrimmed edges (*Ancre* somewhat similar to Briquet 485, Padua 1547 and *Main* similar to Briquet 11154, Palermo 1482), ff. i + 196 + i; 307 × 215 (215–227 × 168–180) mm. 1²⁴(as suggested by paired presence and absence of watermarks, − the first 2 leaves and the last leaf, after f. 29; + an inserted gathering of 8 leaves, ff. 18–25) 2²⁶(− 10 after f. 38) 3²² 4–8²⁴. 2 catchwords only, at the end of quire 2 (f. 54v) and quire 8 (f. 196v), both enclosed in red frames. "2" in the inner margin of the first leaf of quire 2 (f. 30) may be a quire signature. 2 columns of 32–37 lines, except on ff. 34v–47v (arts. 21, 22) with long lines, and ff. 72v–79 (art. 30) in verse. Ruled in lead; round prick marks in the 3 outer margins. Written in a mixed, predominantly secretary script; rubrics usually in a textura formata script; occasional words written in cipher (e.g. ff. 50, 102v, 111, 143, 163).

Simple illustrations in ink, with hair tinted yellow, of a Vein Man (f. 8v) and 2 Zodiac Men (ff. 12v, 14); urine bottles, not colored in, on ff. 39–47v; diagrams, charts, tables and astrological signs in ink of the text, in red and in yellow wash. 4- to 1-line initials, usually in red only, some in red with crude ink flourishing, some also with a yellow wash (through f. 17); 1-line initials in the text slashed in red; red paragraph marks and some red rubrics. Contemporary foliation shows loss of one leaf after f. 29 and after the present f. 38, both with loss of text; the foliation apparently skipped the numbers 44 and 88, as text and quire structure run continuously.

Bound in 1971 in polished calf; previous binding, s. XVIII, in English calf.

Written in England towards the end of the fifteenth century; computistic cycles in the calendar are dated 1480 and 1520; some of the feasts in the liturgical calendar were instituted in 1480 (Visitation, Frideswide, Etheldreda); the feast of the Transfiguration was instituted in England in 1487; on f. 72 is a mention of Henry VII, showing that part of the text to be written in 1485 or later. Names of early owners are: s. XV^{ex} or XVI^{in}: ff. 82v, 106, 109, 120, 140, 149, "Iste liber est [or "constat"] Iohannis eccam [or "ekam"]"; f. 41, possibly in the same hand as "Iohannis eccam," "Caucio Iohannis p'ener alias halpyn pro vi s."; f. 11, "Iohn Han[?]"; s. XVI^{in}: f. 155, "Iohn wallton"; s. XVI$^{in \ or \ med}$: f. 196v, "Hughe drapere merchaunt"; s. XVI: ff. 74, 76v, 81, 160v, "Iohn Bosgrove" (on f. 81, "Iohn Bosgrove ys a mytte man and man of the lerneing wythall"). Said in the Rosenbach description in Library files to have belonged to Dr. John Dee (1527–1608), but there is no evidence of this in the manuscript; the book does not appear in Dee's catalogue, nor is it accepted by R. J. Roberts and A. G. Watson, eds., *John Dee's Library Catalogue* (London, The Bibliographical Society, forthcoming). Bought ca. 1833 by Sir Thomas Phillipps; his MS 6883. Acquired privately through A. S. W. Rosenbach by Henry E. Huntington in 1923.

Bibliography: De Ricci, 48. W. J. Wilson, "Catalogue of Latin and Vernacular Alchemical Manuscripts in the United States and Canada," *Osiris* 6 (1939) 408–18 with plate of f. 17. L. MacKinney, *Medical Illustrations in Medieval Manuscripts* (Berkeley 1965) 148.1. *Aspects of Medieval England,* n. 46 open at f. 14.

APPENDIX 6.

TAGGED MARC RECORD (PARTIAL) FOR HUNTINGTON LIBRARY, HM 64

[Notes in the order prescribed by AACR2r, ch.4.]

[Fixed field omitted; 0XX control fields omitted]

245 00   Astrological and medical compilation.

260 1 $c [not before 1480]

300   196 leaves (2 columns, 32-37 lines), bound; $b paper: $c 31 cm.

500   In Latin, English, and French.

500   Title from Huntington catalog.

541   Acquired privately through A.S.W. Rosenbach by Henry Huntington in 1923.

561   Names of early owners are: (late 15th or early 16th cent.) ff. 82v, 106r, 109r, 120r, 140r, 149r, "Iste liber est [or "constat"] Iohannis eccam [or "ekam"]"; f. 41r, possibly in the same hand as "Iohannis eccam," "Caucio Iohannis p'ener alias halpyn pro vi s."; f. 11r, "Iohn Han[?]"; (early 16th cent.) f. 155r, "Iohn wallton"; (early or mid 16th cent.) f. 196v, "Hughe drapere merchaunt"; (16th cent.) ff. 74r, 76v, 81r, 160v, "Iohn Bosgrove" (on f. 81r, "Iohn Bosgrove ys a mytte man and man of the lerneing wythall"). Said in the Rosenbach description in the Library files to have belonged to Dr. John Dee, but there is no evidence of this in the manuscript and the book does not appear in Dee's catalog. Bought ca. 1833 by Sir Thomas Phillipps; his MS 6883.

500   Written in England towards the end of the fifteenth century; computistic cycles in the calendar are dated 1480 and 1520; some of the feasts in the litugical calendar were instituted in 1480 (Visitation, Frideswide, Etheldreda); the feast of the Transfiguration was instituted in England in 1487; on f. 72r is a mention of Henry VII, showing that part of the text to be written in 1485 or later.

506   Access restricted.
555 8   Described in: Guide to Medieval and Renaissance Manu-
           scripts in the Huntington Library (Huntington Library,
           1989).
510 4   Ricci, $c p. 48
510 4   Wilson, W.J. "Catalogue of . . . Alchemical Manu-
           scripts." Osiris 6 (1939): 408-418
510 4   MacKinney, Medical Illustrations, $c 148.1
510 4   Aspects of Medieval England, $c 46
510 4 $3 2 $a Walther. Initia, $c 14721
510 4 $3 2 $a Walther. Initia, $c 145623
510 4 $3 10 $a Schuler, R.M. English Magical and Scientific
           Poems to 1700, $c 60
510 4 $3 10 $a Hanna, R. "Index of Middle English Verse . . .
           Addenda." PBSA 74 (1980): 235-58, $c 6
510 4 $3 23 $a Walther. Initia, $c 8211
510 4 $3 15 $a Thorndike-Kibre, 42

. . . . [additional citations referring to individual works omitted
   here]. . . .

524   Huntington Library, HM 64.
500   Includes: 1. Explanations of tables (f. 1r-2r) — 2. Calendar
           (ff. 2r-7v) — 3. Tables of indications (f. 8r) — 4. Table
           of ascendancy of planets (f. 8v) — 5. Vein man (ff. 8v-
           10v); Ad minuendum sanguinem (f. 9r) — 6. Canon
           signorum (f. 10v-11r) — 7. Blank pages ruled for table
           of eclipses (ff. 11v-12r) — 8. Homo signorum (f. 12v) —
           9. Table to determine when the sun enters a sign of the
           zodiac (f. 13r) — 10. Table of relationships between the
           4 elements and the 12 signs of the zodiac (ff. 13v-14r);
           zodiac man (f. 14r) — 11. Ad sciendum gradus siccitatis
           et caliditatis (f. 14v) — 12. Hic incipit canon et figura
           spere (ff. 14v-16v) — 13. Ad cognossendum pulsum ali-
           cuius (ff. 16v-17r) — 14. World map (f. 17r) — 15. Ex-
           cerpts in English from Ps.-Aristoteles, Secreta secre-
           torum (f. 17v) — 16. Charms (ff. 17v, 21v, 34r,
           51r) — 17. Galieni medici Regimen sanitatis feliciter in-
           cipit (ff. 18r-21v) — 18. Medical recipes and dietary

recommendations in English (ff. 22r-25v) — 19. Excerpts from the work of Johannes Jacobi (ff. 26r-26v) — 20. Portions of 2 treatises commonly called Trotula minor (ff. 28v-34r) — 21. Medical recommendations mainly in Latin (ff. 34v-38v) — 22. Treatise on urine (ff. 38v-50r) — 23. Here bygynnythe the tokenys that Ipocrace the goode leche wrote . . . (ff. 50r-51r)

500   24. Recipes in English and Latin (f. 51r-v) — 25. Here Begynnes the booke of astronomye and of philosofye . . . (ff. 52r-61v) — 26. Text on the four humors (ff. 61v-62) — 27. Text of prescription of laxatives taken at different time of the year (ff. 62r-63r) — 28. Text on male and female complexions as determined by birth dates and influence of the zodiac (ff. 63r-72r) — 29. Notes on the use of arabic and roman numerals and a brief chronology from the origin of the world to the seventh year of King Henry after the Conquest (f. 72r) — 30. *The right Pitte of helle is amydys the erthe withein* . . . (f. 72v-79r) — 31. *Septem sunt planete secundum dicta philosophorum* . . . (f. 79r) — 32. Here saythe Galianus the goode leche that was of metis and dryngkis to use in tyme of the yere . . . (ff. 79v-81r) — 33. Seven medical recipes in English (f. 81r) — 34. Text on perilous days (ff. 81v-83r) — 35. Six medical recipes in English (f. 83r) — 36. [Storia lune] *Gode that all this worlde wroughte* . . . (ff. 83v-93v) — 37. Four medical recipes in English (f. 93v) — 38. Calendarial prognostics in English (ff. 94r-95r) — 39. Two medical recipes in English (f. 95r) — 40. Tractatus mirabilis aquarum quas composuit Petrus Hispanensis . . . (ff. 95v-101r) — 41. Approximately 20 recipes (ff. 101v-103r)

500   42. English translation of a portion of Petrus Hispanus, Liber de oculo (ff. 103r-104r) — 43. Approximately 120 recipes, mostly in English (ff. 104r-113r) — 44. Here bygynnys a boke of many medycins for many evilles . . . (ff. 113v-120r) — 45. *Hec sunt semina 4or frigidorum maiorum* . . . (f. 120r) — 46. Approximately 55 gynecological recipes in Latin, each citing a authority

(ff. 120r-121v) — 47. Note on pharmaceutical weights (f. 121v) — 48. Pharmaceutical recipes and surgical procedures (ff. 121v-124v) — 49. Hec incipit quid pro quo (ff. 125r-135r) — 50. Recipes and descriptions of sicknesses in Latin (ff. 135v-138r) — 51. Approximately 60 recipes and charms in English (ff. 138r-143r) — 52. Hic incipit tractatus de virtutibus corei serpentis secundum Iohannem pallium (f. 143r-v) — 53. Approximately 450 medical recipes, mainly in English (ff. 143v-176r) — 54. Agnus castus (ff. 176v-183v) — 55. Glossary of herbs in Latin, with some English and French equivalents (ff. 184r-190v) — 56. Recipes and charms in Latin (ff. 191r-196v) — 57. Medical recipes in English, added in 15th and 16th cent. (ff. 176r, 183v, 184v, 186r, 186r, 187r, 188v, 190r).

500	Edges of paper untrimmed.
500	Watermarks: anchor (somewhat similar to Briquet 485, Padua 1547), and hand (similar to Briquet 11154, Palermo 1482).
500	Written in a mixed, predominantly secretary script; rubrics usually in a textura formata script; occasional words written in cipher.
500	Simple illustrations in ink, with hair tinted yellow, of a vein man (f. 8v) and two zodiac men (ff. 12v, 14r); urine bottles, not colored (ff. 39r-47v); diagrams, charts, tables and astrological signs in ink of the text, in red and in yellow wash; 4- to 1-line initials usually in red only; 1-line initials in the text slashed in red; red paragraph marks and some red rubrics.
500	Collation: 1^{24} (as suggested by paired presence and absence of watermarks, — the first 2 leaves and the last leaf, after f. 29; + an inserted gathering of 8 leaves, ff. 18-25) 2^{26} (-10 after f. 38) 3^{22} 4-8.^{24}
500	2 catchwords only, at the end of quire 2 (f. 54v) and quire 8 (f. 196v), both enclosed in red frames.
500	Ruled in lead; round prick marks in the 3 outer margins.
500	Contemporary foliation shows loss of one leaf after f. 29

and after the present f. 38, both with loss of text; the foliation apparently skipped the numbers 44 and 88, as text and quire structure run continuously.

500   Bound in 1971 in polished calf; previous binding, 18th cent., in English calf.

500    $3 1 $a Est notandum quod in prima linea descendendo versus sinistram scribitur numerus dierum . . .

500    $3 1 $a Postea annectuntur tria tria [sic] cicli coniunccionum et apposicionum verarum Solis et lune . . .

500    $3 5 $a At the auctoritate of Ipsocras the Nobell phesiscion Isodore tellithe that there be e thre dayes in the yere in the whiche men schulde not blede . . .

. . . . [additional incipits omitted here]. . . . .

650 10   Medicine, Medieval.
650 10   Medicine $y 15th-18th centuries.
650 10   Astrology $x Early works to 1800.
650 10   Body fluids $x Early works to 1800.
650 10   Bloodletting $x Early works to 1800.
650 10   Recipes.
650 10   Charms.
655 7   Medical formularies. $2rbgenr
655 7   Calendars. $2rbgenr
700 02   Aristotle, $c Pseudo. $t Secreta secretorum. $k Selections.
700 02   Bartholomaeus, $c de Ferraria. $t De regimine sanitatis.
700 02   Petrus Hispanus. $t Liber de oculo.
700 10   Eccam, John, $e former owner.
700 10   P'ener, John, $e associated name.
700 10   Han, John, $e former owner.
700 10   Wallton, John, $e former owner.
700 10   Draper, Hugh, $e former owner.
700 10   Bosgrove, John, $e former owner.
700 10   Dee, John, $e associated name.
700 10   Phillipps, Thomas, $c Sir, $e former owner.
700 10   Rosenbach, A.S.W., $e associated name.
730 02   Agnus castus.
755   Autographs. $2rbprov

To index this record, apart from free-text searching of the 5XX fields, it will be necessary to (1) establish names and titles, (2) regularise orthography of incipits, and (3) provide index entries in 6XX or 7XX for:

General subjects [650]
Genres of works [655]
Authors names (with titles if appropriate) [700]
Titles traced separately for direct access by title [730 or 740]
Titles of anonymous works [730 or 740]
Incipits traced as titles [740]
Names of previous owners [700]
Physical characteristics of the manuscript [755]

APPENDIX 7.

TAGGED MARC RECORD (PARTIAL)
FOR HUNTINGTON LIBRARY, HM 64

[Notes in the order prescribed by APPM2]

[Fixed field omitted; 0XX control fields omitted]

245 00   Astrological and medical compilation.
260 1 $c [not before 1480]
300   196 leaves (2 columns, 32-37 lines), bound; $b paper: $c 31 cm.
500   Title from Huntington catalog.
500   Includes: 1. Explanations of tables (f. 1r-2r) — 2. Calendar (ff. 2r-7v) — 3. Tables of indications (f. 8r) — 4. Table of ascendancy of planets (f. 8v) — 5. Vein man (ff. 8v-10v); Ad minuendum sanguinem (f. 9r) — 6. Canon signorum (f. 10v-11r) — 7. Blank pages ruled for table of eclipses (ff. 11v-12r) — 8. Homo signorum (f. 12v) — 9. Table to determine when the sun enters a sign of the zodiac (f. 13r) — 10. Table of relationships between the 4 elements and the 12 signs of the zodiac (ff. 13v-14r); zodiac man (f. 14r) — 11. Ad sciendum gra-

dus siccitatis et caliditatis (f. 14v) — 12. Hic incip
canon et figura spere (ff. 14v-16v) — 13. Ad cognosser
dum pulsum alicuius (ff. 16v-17r) — 14. World map (
17r) — 15. Excerpts in English from Ps.-Aristoteles, S(
creta secretorum (f. 17v) — 16. Charms (ff. 17v, 21v
34r, 51r) — 17. Galieni medici Regimen sanitatis felic
ter incipit (ff. 18r-21v) — 18. Medical recipes and d
etary recommendations in English (ff. 22r-25v) — 1!
Excerpts from the work of Johannes Jacobi (ff. 26:
26v) — 20. Portions of 2 treatises commonly called Tr(
tula minor (ff. 28v-34r) — 21. Medical recommend;
tions mainly in Latin (ff. 34v-38v) — 22. Treatise o
urine (ff. 38v-50r) — 23. Here bygynnythe the token)
that Ipocrace the goode leche wrote . . . (ff. 50r-51r)

500   24. Recipes in English and Latin (f. 51r-v) — 25. Here B(
gynnes the booke of astronomye and of philosofye . .
(ff. 52r-61v) — 26. Text on the four humors (ff. 61v
62) — 27. Text of prescription of laxatives taken at di:
ferent time of the year (ff. 62r-63r) — 28. Text on mal
and female complexions as determined by birth date
and influence of the zodiac (ff. 63r-72r) — 29. Notes o
the use of arabic and roman numerals and a brief chrc
nology from the origin of the world to the seventh ye;
of King Henry after the Conquest (f. 72r) — 30. *Th
right Pitte of helle is amydys the erthe withein* . . . (
72v-79r) — 31. *Septem sunt planete secundum dicta ph.
losophorum* . . . (f. 79r) — 32. Here saythe Galianus th
goode leche that was of metis and dryngkis to use i
tyme of the yere . . . (ff. 79v-81r) — 33. Seven medic;
recipes in English (f. 81r) — 34. Text on perilous day
(ff. 81v-83r) — 35. Six medical recipes in English (!
83r) — 36. [Storia lune] *Gode that all this world
wroughte* . . . (ff. 83v-93v) — 37. Four medical recipe
in English (f. 93v) — 38. Calendarial prognostics in Er
glish (ff. 94r-95r) — 39. Two medical recipes in Englis
(f. 95r) — 40. Tractatus mirabilis aquarum quas compc
suit Petrus Hispanensis . . . (ff. 95v-101r) — 41. A؛
proximately 20 recipes (ff. 101v-103r)

500   42. English translation of a portion of Petrus Hispanus, Liber de oculo (ff. 103r-104r) — 43. Approximately 120 recipes, mostly in English (ff. 104r-113r) — 44. Here bygynnys a boke of many medycins for many evilles . . . (ff. 113v-120r) — 45. Hec sunt semina 4or frigidorum maiorum . . . (f. 120r) — 46. Approximately 55 gynecological recipes in Latin, each citing a authority (ff. 120r-121v) — 47. Note on pharmaceutical weights (f. 121v) — 48. Pharmaceutical recipes and surgical procedures (ff. 121v-124v) — 49. Hec incipit quid pro quo (ff. 125r-135r) — 50. Recipes and descriptions of sicknesses in Latin (ff. 135v-138r) — 51. Approximately 60 recipes and charms in English (ff. 138r-143r) — 52. Hic incipit tractatus de virtutibus corei serpentis secundum Iohannem pallium (f. 143r-v) — 53. Approximately 450 medical recipes, mainly in English (ff. 143v-176r) — 54. Agnus castus (ff. 176v-183v) — 55. Glossary of herbs in Latin, with some English and French equivalents (ff. 184r-190v) — 56. Recipes and charms in Latin (ff. 191r-196v) — 57. Medical recipes in English, added in 15th and 16th cent. (ff. 176r, 183v, 184v, 186r, 187r, 188v, 190r).

500   In Latin, English, and French.

561   Names of early owners are: (late 15th or early 16th cent.) ff. 82v, 106r, 109r, 120r, 140r, 149r, "Iste liber est [or "constat"] Iohannis eccam [or "ekam"]"; f. 41r, possibly in the same hand as "Iohannis eccam," "Caucio Iohannis p'ener alias halpyn pro vi s."; f. 11r, "Iohn Han[?]"; (early 16th cent.) f. 155r, "Iohn wallton"; (early or mid 16th cent.) f. 196v, "Hughe drapere merchaunt"; (16th cent.) ff. 74r, 76v, 81r, 160v, "Iohn Bosgrove" (on f. 81r, "Iohn Bosgrove ys a mytte man and man of the lerneing wythall"). Said in the Rosenbach description in the Library files to have belonged to Dr. John Dee, but there is no evidence of this in the manuscript and the book does not appear in Dee's catalog. Bought ca. 1833 by Sir Thomas Phillipps; his MS 6883.

541	Acquired privately through A.S.W. Rosenbach by Henry Huntington in 1923.
506	Access restricted.
555 8	Described in: Guide to Medieval and Renaissance Manuscripts in the Huntington Library (Huntington Library, 1989).
510 4	Ricci, $c p. 48
510 4	Wilson, W.J. "Catalogue of . . . Alchemical Manuscripts." Osiris 6 (1939): 408-418
510 4	MacKinney, Medical Illustrations, $c 148.1
510 4	Aspects of Medieval England, $c 46
524	Huntington Library, HM 64.
500	Written in England towards the end of the fifteenth century; computistic cycles in the calendar are dated 1480 and 1520; some of the feasts in the litugical calendar were instituted in 1480 (Visitation, Frideswide, Etheldreda); the feast of the Transfiguration was instituted in England in 1487; on f. 72r is a mention of Henry VII, showing that part of the text to be written in 1485 or later.
500	Edges of paper untrimmed.
500	Watermarks: anchor (somewhat similar to Briquet 485, Padua 1547), and hand (similar to Briquet 11154, Palermo 1482).
500	Written in a mixed, predominantly secretary script; rubrics usually in a textura formata script; occasional words written in cipher.
500	Simple illustrations in ink, with hair tinted yellow, of a vein man (f. 8v) and two zodiac men (ff. 12v, 14r); urine bottles, not colored (ff. 39r-47v); diagrams, charts, tables and astrological signs in ink of the text, in red and in yellow wash; 4- to 1-line initials usually in red only; 1-line initials in the text slashed in red; red paragraph marks and some red rubrics.
500	Collation: 1^{24} (as suggested by paired presence and absence of watermarks, — the first 2 leaves and the last leaf, after f. 29; + an inserted gathering of 8 leaves, ff. 18-25) 2^{26} (-10 after f. 38) 3^{22} $4\text{-}8^{24}$.

500	2 catchwords only, at the end of quire 2 (f. 54v) and quire 8 (f. 196v), both enclosed in red frames.
500	Ruled in lead; round prick marks in the 3 outer margins.
500	Contemporary foliation shows loss of one leaf after f. 29 and after the present f. 38, both with loss of text; the foliation apparently skipped the numbers 44 and 88, as text and quire structure run continuously.
500	Bound in 1971 in polished calf; previous binding, 18th cent., in English calf.
650 10	Medicine, Medieval.
650 10	Medicine $y 15th-18th centuries.
650 10	Astrology $x Early works to 1800.
650 10	Body fluids $x Early works to 1800.
650 10	Bloodletting $x Early works to 1800.
650 10	Recipes.
650 10	Charms.
655 7	Medical formularies. $2rbgenr
655 7	Calendars. $2rbgenr
700 10	Eccam, John, $e former owner.
700 10	P'ener, John, $e associated name.
700 10	Han, John, $e former owner.
700 10	Wallton, John, $e former owner.
700 10	Draper, Hugh, $e former owner.
700 10	Bosgrove, John, $e former owner.
700 10	Dee, John, $e associated name.
700 10	Phillipps, Thomas, $c Sir, $e former owner.
700 10	Rosenbach, A.S.W., $e associated name.
730 02	Agnus castus.
755	Autographs. $2rbprov

APPENDIX 8.

TAGGED MARC RECORD FOR COMPONENT PART [ITEM 17] OF HUNTINGTON LIBRARY, HM 64

[Fixed field omitted; 0XX control fields omitted]

100 00   Bartholomeus, $c de Ferraria.

245 00   Galieni medici regimen sanitatis feliciter incipit.

260 1 $c [not before 1480]

300   f. 18r-21v: $b paper; $c 31 cm.

580   Part of: Astrological and medical compilation. Huntington Library, HM 64.

500   Attributed by Thorndike-Kibre to Bartholomeus de Ferraria.

510 4   Thorndike-Kibre, $c 1011

510 4   Thorndike-Kibre, $c 1614

506   Access restricted.

555 8   Described in: Guide to Medieval and Renaissance Manuscripts in the Huntington Library (Huntington Library, 1989).

524   Huntington Library, HM 64, f. 18r-21v.

500   Prologue begins: In hoc tractatu et qui intitulantur [sic] de Regimine Sanitatis aliquid Breviter dicendum est cum christo adiutorio de aliquibus.

500   Text begins: De utilitate boni regiminis. Oportet illum qui wlt esse longevus.

650 10   Medicine, Medieval.

700 00   Galen.

740 02   In hoc tractatu et qui intitulantur de Regimine Sanitatis aliquid Breviter dicendum est cum christo adiutorio de aliquibus.

740 02   Oportet illum qui wlt esse longevus.

773 0 $7 [Control subfield determines whether subfield a is indexed] $a Astrological and medical compilation $w [control number of parent record]

APPENDIX 9.

TAGGED MARC RECORD FOR COMPONENT PART [ITEM16] OF HUNTINGTON LIBRARY, HM 64

[Fixed field omitted; 0XX control fields omitted]

245 00   Charms.

260 1 $c [not before 1480]

300   Four leaves; $b paper; $c 31 cm.

580   Forms part of: Astrological and medical compilation. Huntington Library, HM 64.

500   Title from Huntington Library catalog.

520 8   Charms numbered 1-5, consisting of variously formed crosses within inscribed circles.

500   Contents: Contra inimicus [sic], 1 (f. 17v); Contra mortem subitam, 2 (f. 21v); Pro victoria, 3 (f. 34r); Pro Igni, 4 (f. 34v); Contra Demones, 5 (f. 51r).

500   On f. 1r there is a blank circle, with a band for the inscription of a similar charm.

500   On f. 34v, the charm Pro Igni is followed by an additional application against miscarriages.

506   Access restricted.

555 8   Described in: Guide to Medieval and Renaissance Manuscripts in the Huntington Library (Huntington Library, 1989).

524   Huntington Library, HM 64, f. 17v, 21v, 34r, 34v, 51r.

500   $3 Contra inimicus $a Si quis hoc signum super se portat nequid capi ab Inimicus [sic].

500   $3 Contra mortem subitam $a Qui hoc signum super se portat sine confessione non morietur.

500   $3 Pro victoria $a Hoc signum misit deus Regi Tedeon [?] qui cum isto pugnat victoriam habebit.

500   $3 Pro Igni $a Hoc signum crucis portans se non timebis ignem.

500   $3 Pro Igni $a In quacumque domo ubi [the charm] fecerit vel ymago Virginis Dorothee eximie matris [sic] alme, Nullus abortivus infantis nascetur in illa.

500      $3 Contra Demones $a Signum sancti Michaelis quas omnes demones timent die qua videris demones non timebis.

650 10   Charms.

740 02   Si quis hoc signum super se portat nequid capi ab Inimicus.

740 02   Qui hoc signum super se portat sine confessione non morietur.

740 02   Hoc signum misit deus Regi Tedeon [?] qui cum isto pugnat victoriam habebit.

740 02   Hoc signum crucis portans se non timebis ignem.

740 02   In quacumque domo ubi fecerit vel ymago Virginis Dorothee eximie matris alme, Nullus abortivus infantis nascetur in illa.

740 02   Signum sancti Michaelis quas omnes demones timent die qua videris demones non timebis.

773 0 $7 [Control subfield determines whether subfield a is indexed] $a Astrological and medical compilation $w [control number of parent record]

The Future
of Manuscript Cataloguing

Warren Van Egmond

SUMMARY. The author compares the introduction of computers in the twentieth century to the invention of printing in the fifteenth century, noting that scholars in both periods initially saw the new technology only as providing a faster means of doing what they were already doing with existing technology and did not realize its full potential until sometime later. The future of manuscript cataloging will lie in the mass distribution of standardized information, but the existing MARC format for library information will be inadequate to the task of disseminating cataloging information on manuscript books. He encourages the development of special formats for these materials.

Let me begin my response to the papers of Schipke, Amos, and Mayo by saying that medieval and renaissance studies are standing at the beginning of a revolution. It is my conviction that 100, 200, or 300 years from now, when future historians look back upon the decades when electronic computers were first introduced into scholarship, it will seem to them to be a revolution as important as the invention of printing seems to us now when we look back at the events of the late fifteenth century. Today we can look back at that time and see how that new technology revolutionized the scholar's way of gathering, studying, and disseminating information. Instead

Professor Warren Van Egmond has made an extensive study of the manuscript sources for medieval and renaissance mathematics. He is author of *Practical mathematics in the Italian Renaissance*: a Catalog of Italian abbacus manuscripts and printed books to 1600 (Florence 1980). He also served as Assistant Director of the International Computer Catalog of Medieval Scientific Manuscripts at the University of Munich and is currently a lecturer in the University Honors College at Arizona State University.

of painstakingly gathering copies of the texts that he needed, often by copying them himself with all the chances for error that that introduces, he had access to standardized texts that were reproduced in great numbers and circulated throughout Europe with no danger of miscopying. This changed both the way in which he worked with texts and the way he communicated with his colleagues, advancing the process of scholarship in ways that would have been impossible under the previous system.

The introduction of computer technology, I am certain, will have an equally momentous effect on the performance of scholarship in the coming centuries in medieval and renaissance studies as in all other fields, with effects that we cannot yet even foresee. We are the pioneers in this change; we are the people standing on the frontier of this new age. The decisions we make and the work that we do will help to shape the way in which scholarship is done in the future.

The problem is that, like all pioneers, we have no way of truly foreseeing the future. We cannot predict what all the effects of the decisions we make will be; we cannot anticipate all the changes which the introduction of the computer will cause; we cannot really know how scholars will work in the future or what issues will be most important to them. But we can look back to the past to get some idea of the kinds of changes that occurred when an equally new technology was introduced into the world of scholarship in the last half of the fifteenth century.

One thing that stands out is that scholars of the day could not see the importance of what had been invented. The printing press was initially seen simply as a better way to produce copies of manuscript books. Thus the early printers cast their type to duplicate the handwriting styles used in manuscripts; they laid out pages and texts in the same way; they even left spaces for initials to be filled in by the rubricator in the traditional manner of manuscript book production. It wasn't until 50 years or so had passed that scholars began to realize the full potential of printing for producing standardized texts with fixed page and line numbers that could be mass produced and disseminated throughout Europe. At the beginning they saw the printing press only as another way of producing what they were already familiar with — the manuscript book.

Like early scholars facing the printing press, we too have difficulty seeing the computer as anything other than a tool to produce something we are already familiar with—a printed book. At the moment, unable to recognize the computer's full potential or to anticipate the changes it will produce in the way we do our work, we tend to see it as a faster or more convenient way to do what we already do. In the case we are discussing here, this is printing and indexing catalogues of medieval and renaissance manuscripts.

It seems to me that Dr. Renate Schipke's paper illustrates this conservative attitude most clearly. Notice that what she and her colleagues at the Deutsche Staatsbibliothek are doing with the *ZIH* and the *ZIR* is to use the computer to produce a "Zettelkatalog," a card catalogue—basically a nineteenth-century technology. The computer is being used only as a device to produce an index, something that has traditionally been done by writing out cards by hand and sorting them manually. There is no mention in her report of keeping the computer records as a file for future reference, no suggestion of building a database that could be consulted directly by library users or sharing the information with distant users. The project is using a new technology to create an old and familiar device in the same way that the first printers used their new technology to produce manuscripts.

Dr. Thomas L. Amos of the Hill Monastic Manuscript Library, in contrast, has clearly gone a step farther. Although the primary objective of his project is still to produce a printed catalogue (old technology), the Hill Library is planning to develop a computerized database which can be accessed by all users, even those outside the library through telecommunications. This shows an ability to foresee potential future uses of the new technology that should be lauded and encouraged.

It is clearly difficult to escape the idea of using the computer to produce what we are already used to—printed catalogues and indexes. Indeed, is it even possible for people who are trained in the past to see into the future? Can we escape our past habits of thought? Can we foresee the true uses of the computer in the coming decades and centuries? If so, what might they be?

Let me offer a few suggestions. It seems to me most likely that the primary advantage of the computer will be to extend further the same advantages that were introduced by the invention of printing. These are standardization and mass distribution.

Before the invention of printing scholars had great difficulty studying the basic texts. Hand-copied texts had frequent errors and many variations, with the result that there were a number of different versions that could only be referenced in general and imprecise ways. Once the advantages of printing were realized, texts were produced in standard editions with page and line numbers that could be referred to by all scholars. With the ability to reproduce these texts in large numbers without copying errors and to distribute them throughout the world, scholars could research and share ideas more easily.

But printing is not perfect. Printing errors are almost as frequent as copying errors, and mass production only reproduces them in massive quantities. Moreover, once a book has been printed and distributed, there is no way to get new information into it. It cannot be corrected or altered except by printing a new edition which simply starts the whole process over again, or by publishing a long list of errata and addenda which are difficult to use and easily lost. And even though the book can be printed in large quantities, there is still the problem of getting it to the person who needs to use it. For large and specialized works like catalogues of manuscripts, the persistence of errors and difficulty of access continue to plague scholars.

It seems to me that the computer offers the perfect solution to these remaining problems. If all of the information were maintained in a central data bank that was constantly updated and corrected, there would be little danger of perpetuating errors or using outdated information. Any errors could be corrected as soon as they were discovered and new information could be added as it was produced. Furthermore, if such a databank were open to every user through telecommunication links, the problem of limited access would be virtually eliminated. The dream of having the same standardized and current information available to any scholar anywhere in the world at any time would finally be realized.

In order to make this dream a reality however, certain steps must be taken. First, scholars who use original sources in manuscript must agree on the adoption of uniform international standards for the description and dissemination of information, in the same way that computer scientists have agreed on an international code for the exchange of information—the ASCII code. As a consequence of the ASCII code for information exchange, electronic messages can be sent even now between any two connected computers anywhere in the world within minutes. Similarly, librarians have adopted or are adopting the MARC format for exchange of standard cataloguing information about printed books, and many library catalogues are already being placed on computer and opened to external on-line access.

In order to extend these benefits to manuscript materials, we need to develop a similar standard for the description and exchange of manuscript cataloguing information. Widespread use of the MARC standard for library information makes it seem likely that it should also be used for manuscript cataloguing, but can manuscript descriptions be fitted into the MARC format? The problem is that manuscripts are fundamentally different in character from printed books and require a significantly different set of cataloguing criteria.

Dr. Hope Mayo has done a magnificent job of trying to make the two fit, and I applaud her efforts. But she reports two major difficulties: most manuscripts contain multiple texts on diverse subjects, with more than one work copied or bound into a single volume, whereas the MARC format, like most book cataloguing systems, assumes that a printed book will contain only one work or a collection of works dealing with a single theme. There seems to be no efficient way to list such texts individually in the MARC system. Similarly, the listing of incipits and explicits is essential for the identification of all manuscripts, but there is no provision for such a category in the MARC format. Without facilities for these two things, as well as provision for the many other categories used in the best modern protocols for describing manuscripts, it does not seem to me that the MARC format is suitable for manuscript catalogues. It is possible that solutions can be found, for example by cataloguing in terms of individual texts instead of an entire manuscript, or by creating a specialty field within the MARC system. But it is clear that any such solutions will be awkward to use and would remain ad hoc additions to a system that was never intended to incorporate such uses.

In my view, attempting to mold the MARC format to suit the needs of medieval and renaissance scholars who search for and analyse manuscript sources is a fruitless endeavor. I believe we should instead go ahead and develop our own standards that are specifically designed to meet our needs as cataloguers and users of manuscripts and then let the librarians themselves worry about how to incorporate our catalogues into theirs, if at all. One way the two approaches could be melded is to provide the library catalogues with a short-hand, first-level description of author, title, and location of text in manuscript and then include a reference to a specialized manuscript catalogue for those who wish to investigate further.

Whatever solution is eventually found, it is clear that the world of scholarship is going to change in ways we can only dimly foresee. It is up to us, to our generation, to set the standards and patterns that future scholars will be using for generations to come. We have a chance to shape the future, if only we can see it clearly enough.

Manuscripts and Informatics: Progress and Prospects

Lawrence J. McCrank

SUMMARY. Medieval and renaissance scholars are now using computers increasingly to prepare inventories and even more complex descriptions, but they are mechanizing previous manual processes rather than taking full advantage of automation, new bibliographic utilities and networks, and the recent development of information systems. Nevertheless, there have been some interesting applications in computer-generated conventional reference tools for access to manuscript resources which point to the development of interactive data bases capable of access in machine-readable form through established library and archival information systems.

The greatest barrier to humanistic research across cultural boundaries provided by natural language texts or by diversity of pictorial images has been the lack of authority control, standard protocols, format guidelines, and financing of online searching outside one's own institution. Mechanisms are now available for sharing such in-

Lawrence J. McCrank, PhD, MLS, is Dean of Library and Instructional Services at Ferris State University, Big Rapids, Michigan. He previously served in the same capacity at Auburn University at Montgomery and as Head of the Department of Rare Books and Special Collections at Indiana State University. At the University of Maryland, College Park, he designed and implemented the award-winning double masters programs in History and Library Science with specialization in Archives Administration. He has been Visiting Professor in Information Studies at the Universities of Alabama, Western Ontario, and Wayne State, and of History at the Universities of Oregon and California (Berkeley), and Western Michigan.

As author or editor of more than a dozen monographs, he has also published 50 articles in journals here and abroad. Dr. McCrank's historical research foci are on the medieval frontier of Reconquest Spain, monastic studies and acculturation, and on parallel topics in the American West. His interests in archival science and rare books and manuscripts have focused on automation, preservation, bibliography control, diplomatics, codicology, and analytical bibliography.

159

formation via bibliographic networks using the international MARC standard (Machine-Readable Cataloging). Other technical developments allow for the transfer of visual images that are retrievable with textual data.

The relatively new MARC Archives and Manuscripts Cataloging (AMC) may provide adequate means for codicological description, because its linking capabilities allow for the subordination of descriptive fields, full-text and tabular descriptions, and manuscript collations in matrix form (the so-called Delaissé method). These efforts are discussed along with the evolving standards within the Anglo-American descriptive tradition, to suggest ways in which descriptive practices by codicologists and related manuscript scholars might have reciprocal influence on the standards used in bibliographic networking for sharing manuscript information.

It once seemed premature if not inhumane to hope for computer applications to facilitate access to primary sources in manuscript. With so many medieval and renaissance manuscripts lacking even a bare inventory or preliminary cataloguing, machine readable catalogues which would include descriptive data of any serious complexity appeared to be the fantasy of science fiction. On the other hand the older manual approaches to manuscript description were outdated and could not be usefully imitated, and the standards for traditional manuscript cataloguing have been quite uncertain.

The papers presented at the ICHS Symposium, however, have shown that such limitations are no longer necessary. Information technology has progressed so that hopes of past decades are becoming realities, while the newer manuscript catalogues are displaying higher descriptive standards. The potential of ready access to original documents and primary sources in manuscript with assistance of computers has been greatly improved in a single decade. And it should be emphasised also that current trends hold ever greater promise for scholarly research.[1] Scholars should place greater value, therefore, with new scholarship in medieval and renaissance studies, on new means for access to original sources for these studies.

Computer applications to medieval text and data analysis began with word counts and concordances. In some cases like the numerous works of Saint Bernard and Saint Thomas Aquinas, those initial applications of informatics allowed some advantages for the study of every imaginable permutation of words or turn of phrase for a few authors. But current informatics provides research methods and techniques (especially in expert systems design) which are appropriate for the intellectual control of literary material and could provide much better access to library documents or archives which enable better access to and further analysis of medieval primary sources, whether in code form or loose manuscripts.

When access to original sources was comparatively difficult for most humanistic scholars, generalizations drawn from the best printed texts or from such few manuscripts as might be locally available were all that could be had. But after a century of examining the most famous texts, standard editions, and key manuscripts, history and literary analysis have turned from grand theory and overarching designs to reinterpretation and revision, color and detail, exploration of new discoveries in what were once peripheral subjects, and revealing in-depth studies of matters too easily accepted. Minutia not previously comprehensible are being examined in many different contexts, resulting in new interpretations, theoretical structures, and significant revisionism. Such scholarship requires intellectual access far more precise, with greater recall, and infinitely more documentary scope than was previously made available by author/short-title catalogs, inventories and registers, or other finding aids for each institution. Such new and much more sophisticated finding aids have been created recently by humanistic scholars, individually or in groups, and sometimes by institutes and libraries, with the assistance of computers.

Customized design of new tools requires expertise beyond traditional approaches to manuscript studies.[2] Derived from bio-medical fields, the neologism "informatics" is sometimes used to combine information science and technology for a systems approach to information storage and retrieval or referral (ISAR).[3] In less empirical French usage, "informatique" is used almost synonymously with applied information science. Information systems consist of a data base, communication mode, a methodology for intellectual control, the adaptation of a technology or set of techniques and tools such as a DBMS software package, and documentation. In some systems it is important to link the descriptive record or surrogate with the original for the purpose of proof, as in the case of archives, museums, and libraries devoted to primary sources or special collections. Consequently, informatics is an umbrella term encompassing a great purview in the information field; it is an approach rather than any single system, applicable to many disciplines and data, which may involve bibliographic information. The focus of this discussion is the overlap, interplay, and commonality between two knowledge domains, information science and its applied subfields of librarianship and archival administration, with manuscript studies and their requirements for codicology as well as content analysis. In addition there must be attention to past progress and continuing problems in the intellectual access to medieval and renaissance manuscripts (Hausmann, *et alii*, 1987).

DESCRIPTION AND CATALOGUING

There has been much recent work by librarians and archivists on access to early manuscripts and rare books which would be useful to review. Many aspects of manuscript cataloguing were highlighted by the Wolfenbüttel conference on problems of handling medieval manuscripts (Härtel, 1986), considering the 1983 third revised edition of cataloguing rules for manuscript codices (Winter, Schipke, and Teitge, 1983). This included the standardization of descriptors and the possibility of computerization, but it did not venture into the more complicated issue of subject access and relation between document retrieval and analytics (Leonhard, 1985). Collaborative cataloguing and conservation projects at the Herzog August Library in Wolfenbüttel, the Bavarian State Library in Munich, and other great libraries promoted institutional cooperation within national boundaries.

But during the 1980s there was also increased awareness of the need for international standards. The English Short Title Catalogue (ESTC) and the North American Imprints (NAIP) had raised similar questions about international bibliography (Snyder, 1979). Revision of the Anglo-American Cataloguing Rules had likewise turned specialist attention to standards for the cataloguing of rare books (Library of Congress, 1981) and about short-form citations for referral to standard bibliographic tools (Van Wingen and Douglas, 1982). The useful work of G. T. Tanselle in analytical bibliography

(1974, 1979) can be applied to these issues, although there are few tools that are as directly applicable to medieval codices (Needham, 1979; Etherington and Roberts, 1982). Internationally there was a revised standard for the description of antiquarian materials (ISBD/A) and what was heralded as major developments in the international world of rare book librarianship (Wilson, 1956). However, much of the medieval and renaissance manuscript work is outside usual librarianship, and the two fields of modern bibliography and manuscript codicology seem to have coexisted with little rapport and little recognition of mutual problems. Indeed, the literature talks more about convergent technology than about convergence in methodology, standards, and the professions.

One might have wished for more progress toward information exchange between these fields. But there is a variety of conventions, preferred formats for presentation, descriptive "standards or persuasions, and a certain coalescence toward standards in several manuscript catalogues representative of the last one and one-half decades." This is true for Armenian manuscripts in the U.S. (Sanjian, 1976); Waddeston Manor (Delaissé, Parkes, and Marrow, 1977); University of Notre Dame (Corbett, 1978); Keble College (Parkes, 1979); Hispanic Society of America (Faulhaber, 1983); Beinecke Library at Yale (Shailor, 1984); Library of Congress (Schutzner, 1989); Newberry Library (Saenger, 1989); the Huntington Library (Dutschke, 1989); Utrecht University's library (Van der Horst, 1990); and ongoing projects elsewhere. Those stressing illumination show the influence of Delaissé's layout; those largely text adhere more closely to older formats. Scholarly standards have been high, but approaches, formats, conventions, and presentations have been traditional; and computer applications are largely confined to text-processing and assistance in book production.[4]

Unlike collections of manuscripts assembled for their art which are often homogeneous, librarians are aware that texts are heterogeneous and that archival materials are more different still. Barbara Shailor's excellent catalogue (1984) of the Beinecke Library's codices encompassed such a heterogeneous lot. She thus faced a wide range of choices for her descriptions and formats and, although not the first to use electronic means for publications, her work was caught in the transition when conventions for handling machine-readable files of such material were not well established. Her observations then are still relevant today: "The matter of suitable format for cataloguing medieval and renaissance manuscripts is a difficult one since there are few firmly established guidelines" (Shailor, 1984, p. xviii). In the absence of genuine standards for the descriptive cataloguing of manuscripts, she struggled with the criteria: . . . "first, to note accurately the textual contents and physical makeup of the fragment or codex; second, to relate briefly the material . . . to manuscripts preserved elsewhere; third, to serve as a point of departure for further inquiry by scholars and collectors." Her dilemma was not unlike that of Albert Gruijs' attention to "bare essentials" and "registration of immutable facts." Each cataloguer has had to define his or her own standards.

This lack of standardization is illustrated in a variety of methods for manuscript transcription which also vary by school, without having yet coalesced into the kind of specific systems available for transcription (Weijers, 1989). M. P. Brown (p. 5), for example, chooses a "conflation of the 'Leiden' system, devised for papyrological and epigraphic use (Turner, 1968), and of the *Scriptorium* system, again a modification of the inventions of Julian Brown. These conventions work; but other conventions work as well, better for some scholars than for others. There is no single, right way, and indeed no system at all when matters of transcription and script nomenclature remain largely a matter of individual taste.

Manuscript cataloguing relying on this convention or that nevertheless needs to be re-formulated or even to be translated when read by a scholar. But when such information is prepared for machine-readable transfer, catalogue entries all require extensive editing. This is the case for most extant descriptive cataloguing of manuscripts. The lack of standards in codicological scholarship now seems to require a massive retrospective conversion project before machine-readable cataloguing and international information transfer can be achieved.

Such a conclusion might be reached if one were committed to editing all cataloguing up to standard before tagging data elements and transferring entries into a machine-readable format. For this purpose should one accept MARC in one national version or another: USMARC for the United States; UKMARC for Great Britain; CANMARC for Canada; IberoMARC for Spain? Or should one turn to Universal Machine-Readable Cataloguing (UNIMARC: Attig, 1983)?[5]

One assumption in using MARC for manuscripts is that the monograph format would be used. But it must be noted that a serial-based format is more accommodating of archival compilations of bound documents and literary extracts with multiple *tituli*.[6] The National Information Systems Task Force of the Society of American Archivists (SAA-NISTF) adopted the serial format for archival series, and that resulted in the MARC-AMC format (Archives and Manuscript Cataloguing) (Sahli, 1985) which received MARBI(ALA) approval. The MARC-AMC also has a set of companion tools such as a cataloguing manual (Hensen, 1983; rev. ed., 1989) and a list of data elements or *A Dictionary of Standard Terminology* (Sahli, 1985).

Whereas archival and intellectual control tend to be divorced in manuscript catalogues, except for the inclusion of shelf marks or call numbers, these were fused in the AMC format. Therefore rare book librarians and codicologists might pay attention to NISTF's accomplishments and organizational procedures. A task force approach moreover resulted in a series of reports and documents to which specialists and professional organizations could react and form consensus.

The SAA-NSTIF success (Lytle, 1984) contains several other lessons for manuscript scholars. First, the series record introduces the idea of multiple descriptive records rather than a single, revised cataloguing entry. Thus, by use of MARC-AMC one can trace the genealogy of an archival collection, the evolution of its intellectual control, and the development of the current description, attributions, and critical appraisal — more than provenance in the sense of ownership. Apart from the source itself, one might want to create a critical apparatus showing the "historical evolution" of the ideal catalogue copy (Stalker, 1990, p. 12), that is, the codicological record which acts as an interpretive guide to past scholarship. Successive linked records act as a critical apparatus and reference system, and not all of these records need to be uniformly complete. It is possible for example to use a short-title catalogue approach to create a "boiler plate" record and to link this with other records that provide more information and fuller descriptions. A manuscript codex of multiple works could have a MARC record for the codex itself and also a series of MARC records for separate "books" contained in the manuscript. Records in a series, perhaps operating like hypertext or hypermedia card stacks, would in effect become an index of *tituli*, incipits, etc., thus creating a very dynamic kind of tool in contrast to static entries now required in book catalogues of most libraries. Such an approach makes it possible to use "phased cataloguing" techniques (McCrank, 1984, pp. 36-37) by which new cataloguing information could be transferred through international bibliographic systems without waiting for the attempted definitive description, thus avoiding a syndrome that has thwarted the effectiveness of union catalogues and has delayed intellectual control over medieval and renaissance manuscripts.

Turning to prospects for future cataloguing: with current technology available to informatics it is also possible to accept the cataloguing format and data first disseminated in book catalogues and to use it in serial or other formats. Without extensive editing and reformatting an existing record in the form of a card catalogue may be scanned optically for creation of a MARC record. A distant researcher may copy the MARC main entry, use its reference notes, and call for backup information from a repository through a variety of mechanisms: reprographic copies or copied diskettes sent through traditional Interlibrary Loan networks; telefacsimile and electronic mail; or some mode of online access to an institution's Online Public Access Catalogue (OPAC) or a host such as the RLIN Research Information Management Program (Hume, 1989) which accommodates the Benjamin Catalogue for History of Science (Hahn, 1991). The major obstacle to such an approach may not be technical but legal, as an issue of copyright and the status of original cataloguing as an intellectual property.[7]

If codicological data were captured in the MARC format on CD-ROM and WORM discs which follow standards for transportability across systems, then resources can easily be shared on- and off-line between institutions, as data bases and mounted on locally hosted systems. But automated library software for mounting multiple data bases need not be MARC formatted: such tools can range from commercially available bibliographic indexes licensed for multiple access to customized data bases such as converting telephone directories back to their electronic forms for searching as personal name indexes. Customized cataloguing tools such as nonstandard manuscript catalogues, pre-MARC work, and other presentations can be thus accommodated by online public access catalogues. Finally, there are catalogues now that access images, very useful for photographic collections, architecture, and art in non-textual forms, either through digitization or through parallel access to analog forms. By such means, not only catalogue descriptions, but transcriptions and facsimiles can be conveyed electronically to workstations in the library and in the scholar's office or home.

EXPERT SYSTEMS AND AUTHORITY CONTROL

The key to systematic information retrieval across diverse systems is authority control for authors, personal names, place names, and uniform titles that collate variants. In modern thesaurus construction one does not have to eliminate variants in subordinating them to a preferred term. Free-text searching for a specific variant is possible and desirable for certain searches; but it is also advantageous to search with terms that act as nets or filters, to gather types of data and information that is already structured.

Extensive bibliographic work in medieval and renaissance studies has already resulted in controls for major authors, including forms of entry, and biographic identification by such qualifiers as titles and dates. Unfortunately the *Anglo-American Cataloging Rules II* allow main entries to by-pass such rigorous identification, and the Library of Congress name authority indexes are inadequate for lesser known medieval and renaissance authors. Such tools are virtually useless for unknown authors, except for the proper syntax in constructing a new author data element.

Medieval onomastics can be perplexing, seemingly defying precise identification or normalization based on modern conventions, but recent advances in prosopographical expert systems are truly impressive (Bourlet & Minel, 1989; Krópac & Becker, 1989). These methods can be applied to systems to maintain name authority controls. There are common conventions for double-entries for personal names and the collation of formal entries, as in the case of a cleric who authored works under a personal name or has works attributed to him, but who assumed a different official name when, for example, becoming pope. The scholar searching a machine readable catalogue of manuscripts which hopefully could contain primary sources for his research project would want to sweep through its data base once, gathering citations of all works by and attributed to a person, without searching the same data base repeatedly with multiple names. The common conventions which would establish authority control for names do not violate the integrity of original data. Despite the ideal, such conventions have not become standards for manuscript cataloguing. They will have to be applied strictly when such catalogue records are entered into bibliographic networks that require certain levels of authority control.

The same problem exists for titles of course for quasi-titles and incipits in manuscript originals, and for those attributed titles which have arisen from later publications. Medievalists still prefer precise transcription and incipit retrieval, despite the problems in information gathering from incipit files due to orthographic variance, formulaic language, and plagiarism (Hamesse, 1990). Incipit retrieval usually depends on key words within the incipit as in the case of title searching, but it cannot be so rigid as to expect normalized syntax. Incipits notoriously vary in their graphics or word order, but there is software (Brately and Hamesse, 1990) that breaks words into diagrammes and searches within pre-set parameters for precision. This allows a searcher to stipulate the degree of variance to expand or contract recall by controlling the precision of the request. Such approaches have been successfully applied in the Louvain Data Base for Incipits of the Manuscripts of the Middle Ages (Hamesse, 1990). Moreover, incipit retrieval like title searching, as simple word matching, lacks the power of term coordination and clustering into sets creating by term subordination and authority control which is the advantage of uniform titles and normalization of names. Such retrieval also lacks the power of provenance which can enhance subject searching.

The most powerful search strategies in bibliographic and codicological retrieval are combinations of standardized term and name searches, uniform titles, truncated term searches for variants, and resort to tagged data elements. Targeting searches for specific locales and periods is important, especially in creating large sets to establish a commonality and then isolating subsets for comparison and contrast. Finally, there are advantages to search bibliographic databases that have been structured, edited, and controlled for ease in information retrieval, but to be able to break from the boundaries created through such standardization and control by free and full-text searching.

Subject access is enhanced through controlled vocabularies or terminologies, but there are few experiments in medieval manuscript description (my own early work during the late 1970s is a notable exception: McCrank, 1983a, 1983b) related to subject access. Nor are there many advances in indexing manuscripts for subject access; a notable program is MEDIUM (a relational database managed system) employed be the Centre National de Recherche Scientifique, Paris, for its IRHT collections of manuscript (original and in microform). Since then there has been some progress in standardized descriptors for rare books in general (ACRL-RBMS, 1983, 1988a, 1989b; IFLA, 1975), bibliographic control (Davis, 1987; Flannery, 1986; LC, 1981; Thomas, 1987), and medieval and renaissance manuscripts in particular (Bischoff *et alii*, 1954 for scripts; Beit-Arie, 1981 for Hebrew mss.; Muzerelle, 1985; and Weijers, 1989).

It is very difficult to control a multi-faceted, multi-cultural and multi-lingual field as complicated as medieval and renaissance studies where subjects existed before evolution of natural language norms and distinctions, the basic principles of naming and classification, standardized orthography, or such advanced techniques as bibliographic control by authors, titles, dates and place of publication, or uniform texts. Codicological controls therefore must allow for customization and control of greater variance than modern bibliographic control has provided. The cataloguing standards for printed material cannot be adopted for the cataloguing of primary sources in manuscript without considerable modification and expansion. However, such changes need to be done within a tradition of control and linked to bibliographic standards, as in the case of archives and library methodology. The two need not be identical to be compatible. Sameness is not the goal; coordination is.

Expert systems are being used increasingly for general reference work (McCrank, 1991b). They should be employed also for research reference. They can be employed for identification and in creating inventory and intellectual controls for manuscripts, and thus also for retrieval. Even relatively simple programs like *Pointer* (SUNY-Buffalo) may be emulated in locating government documents, or *Answerman* for reference, or systems like *Procite* or front-end search directories to catalogues, and more heuristic systems like *Prospector* with its reliance on geographic and geologic data.

Expert systems are a branch of Artificial Intelligence (AI) research that rely on inference, sequential logic, and probability; they relate a query to a precoordinated database, often using language controls, and operating with a shell software. Many expert systems progress on a logic like "if that, then this" through a branching design from the general to the specific (Riggs, Aluri, 1989). They have tremendous potential for historical research, and hence in creating authority control for manuscripts that are not related through previous research to an intellectual structure, established thesaurus, name index, or other tool (McCrank, 1990-91; Schurer, 1990). Several creative methodologies have evolved for prosopography and new social historical research where the subjects are common men and women whose names from original sources like census records would not be known in a reference tool or catalogue. Older applications in the U.S. began during the 1970s by matching routines collating data from large data archives, as in urban studies where addresses from tax lists could be matched with health records, census records, etc. to produce very interesting results in the first wave of so-called quantitative history (Hersberg, 1973, 1980). Such studies were largely limited to numerical data sets, then adapted to standardized text as in the case of personal names and locations within one language. Slowly, such applications have expanded to encompass more varied records, textbases, and sources where language is not so standardized.

There are expert systems which have been developed for use with natural language records in all the variations of several languages, as in the case of medieval and early modern prosopographical studies (Geuenich, 1988; Bourlet & Minel, 1989; Krópac, 1989). There are effective programs for computerized cartulary analysis (Krópac, 1989) which could be applied as well to literary codices to relate content with form, components to the whole, and original sources to the relevant critical literature. With discipline-oriented software such as KLEIW (Thaller, 1987; Smets, 1990), one can expect broader applications of expert systems, the evolution of a new hermeneutics, and a burgeoning field of heuristic tools for improved access to primary sources in the Humanities.

CONCLUSION

We should no longer be using computing merely to produce printed catalogues; manual tools should be spin-off products and adjuncts to automated information systems, not *vice versa*.

There is a real need for informatics to be used to assist scholarly access to primary sources in manuscript to a greater extent than most libraries now provide. Decision-support varieties of expert systems could be used in conjunction with archival and bibliographic control in the construction of locator tools, name lists, thesauri, and linkage between manuscript records, manuscript codices, and artifacts. These could be linked to controls of the secondary literature in the field through bibliographies, indexes, and online catalogues.

There are model projects which should be studied in the design of such systems for codicological and bibliographic studies. One of the most creative is *Project Emperor I* (Chen, 1989) which combines image retrieval frame by frame through indexing as well as "moving pictures" in video, with archeological surveys, still frames, and detail shots, with oral histories and interviews with scholars as well as accompanying textbases. In imitation of the "archeology of the book" idea (Gruijs, 1972; Derolez, 1973), similar comparison is needed for archeological projects (Oikawa, 1989) that combine textbases, indexes and catalogues, image bases, with more conventional library methods.

Major manuscript cataloguing projects today should flourish in these areas of critical analysis of contents and dynamic intellectual access to primary sources.[8] Current applications of information technology, its adoption by archives, museums, and libraries, will make manuscript studies most effective.

NOTES

1. This essay may be read as a continuation of pleas made in 1983 and 1985 for a "continuum of description" and planning for a holistic approach to the enumerative and analytic bibliographic control of primary sources for humanistic research (McCrank, 1985, pp. 204-205).

2. Jacqueline Hamesse (1990) outlined the problem this way at the International Congress of Historical Sciences in Madrid: "The importance of data processing for bibliographical research has made considerable progress during the past decade. Databases, automated information research, direct bibliographical questionings have developed everywhere and in all domains. Nonetheless, despite this considerable progress in historical and documentary research, a sector important for those working on ancient and medieval texts has not experienced the same leaps forward. We are talking about the treatment of manuscripts. For twenty years we have been thinking about the help of the computer in describing and identifying these documents. Various attempts have been made; [some] partially, and localized projects have seen the light of day. But until now, no international cooperation has been set up, no cohesive project has succeeded in organizing these partial enterprises, no agreement has really been implemented in order to homogenize data acquisition, nor to standardize description criteria, nor to plan the stages which would permit automating the description of all manuscript material.

. . . Heuristics in this domain are difficult: nonexistent or insufficient manuscript catalogues in numerous libraries; unpublished or poorly done incipient repertories; codicological information which is altogether summary or passed over in silence. In short, historical research is not facilitated in this domain, for the lack of good working instruments."

3. Informatics seems to have been used in English as a technical term in the field of bio-medical information; but it has achieved broader acceptance for application to primary documentation and artifact control, as in the case of David Bearman's *Archives and Museum Informatics* (1987-), cf. rev., McCrank, (1990), among others.

4. The influence of Fr. Leonard Boyle and Prof. Richard Rouse, through students and consultancies for several cataloguing projects in North America, is pervasive. Authority controls are sometimes established simply by imitating an authority. In essence the scholarly standards and formats of book catalogues undertaken in the United States owe much to Rouse's leadership. It would seem natural to enlist his support of standards formation in a more deliberate effort, whereby subsequent catalogues are improved by such standards, rather than relying on the *status quo* where standards are slowly evolving in the production of catalogues.

5. MARC is used in twenty countries now, and there are at least four union MARC projects. Consequently, it is often assumed (McCrank, 1989) that MARC is a *vademecum* of the international library community for the transfer of catalogue records; but few manuscript cataloguing projects directed from a codicological perspective have adopted MARC. There seems to be a dichotomy between individual scholars cataloguing with their own conventions and preferences and institutional projects which attempt to institutionalize its catalogues and adopt national standards such as AACR-II and its additions.

6. The monograph format may work best for manuscripts of a pre-established form, such as liturgical works. But literary texts were often compiled *ad seriatim* as texts became available, so that even though they may be bound as a codex they are not monographic. In essence many codices resemble a research file of copies, added one at a time, with a rudimentary access system of *tituli*, normalized incipits, rubrication, marginalia, and maybe some kind of table of contents or index added later. Often the critical apparatus of a manuscript is separate from its scribal production, as in the case of binders' "editions."

Forcing such codices into a monographic MARC format does not work very well, although as Hope Mayo demonstrates here, it can be done. This is why some cataloguers think that a special format is required for medieval and renaissance manuscripts (Courthouts, 1987), but this runs counter to the trend toward UNI-MARC or a single comprehensive format that can be adjusted for special formats, rather than having unique formats for every type of media.

7. Consider the implications highlighted by the national controversy in 1989-90 when OCLC considered copyrighting its bibliographic database. In that case the database is a compilation of contributed cataloguing, and the argument was that rights to the data should remain with the originator. This persuasion may seem logical, but it runs counter to copyright law which protects form rather than content, and the publisher rather than the author, unless the author specifically retains copyright. The courts have not yet outlined a clear tradition concerning electronic formats, although there are precedents well established for electronic photocopying which may be applied to scanning and automatic data integration.

The authors of book catalogues already produced and in process have not considered the implications of submitting their work to a copyrighted form. The publishers' rights, and their real need to recover costs for the expensive production of book catalogues that have limited markets, may prohibit the merger of manuscript cataloguing from already published sources into an automated union catalogue. In many cases a publisher will allow the republication of a work by the author without applying fees, but licensing practices are usually unclear about the release of published material into public databases. Because the latter are deliberately intended to make the former obsolescent, there are real grounds for contention in this issue.

8. Such progress is reported in an increased number of conferences devoted to medieval and early modern studies and computing; for example, IVe Congres International "History and Computing" at the Maison des Pays Iberiques, Bordeaux, devoted to Inquisition documentation (Proceedings forthcoming); and its

counterparts in Great Britain surveying the state-of-the-art (Denley and Hopkin, 1990); the ACH-ALLC 91 conference at Arizona State University; Historica 91 (Premieres rencontres nationales sur les applications informatiques à la comprehension de l'histoire) in Paris; and the Centre de Hautes Etudes Internationales d'Informatique Documentaire (CID) in Barcelona (1991), etc. These represent only the announcements of congresses during one quarter of the current year, indicating a pace of activity and project work which is unprecedented. This in itself calls attention to the critical need for standards in automated description, cataloguing, inventory control, and reference systems, as more and more scholars are left to their own devices and preferences in constructing databases for primary sources.

REFERENCES

Abbreviations

ACH	Association for Computers and the Humanities
ACRL	Association of College and Research Libraries
ALA	American Library Association
ALLC	Association for Literary and Linguistic Computing
AMC	Archives and Manuscript Cataloging with MARC
CNR	Centre Nationale du Recherche, Paris
ESTC	English Short Title Catalogue
ICHS	International Congress of Historical Science, Hamburg and Munich, 1-9 August 1989
IFLA	International Federation of Libraries Association
IHRT	Institut d'histoire et recherche du Texte, Paris
ISAR	Information Storage and Retrieval or Referral
ISBD(A)	International Standard Book Description (Antiquarian Books)
MARC	Machine-Readable Cataloging, Library of Congress, Washington, D.C.

CANMARC, Canada
IberoMARC, Spain
MARC-AMC: Archives and Manuscript Cataloging
UNIMARC: Universal Machine-Readable Cataloguing
UKMARC, United Kingdom
USMARC, United States of America

MARBI	Machine-Readable Form of Bibliographic Information (ALA)

NAIP	North American Imprints
NISTF	National Information Systems Task Force of SAA
OCLC	Online Computer Library Catalog Consortium
OPAC	Online Public Access Catalogue
RBMS ACRL	Rare Books and Manuscript Section
RLG	Research Libraries Group, Stanford, California
RLIN	Research Libraries Information Network
SAA	Society of American Archivists

WORKS CITED

ACRL. Rare Books and Manuscript Section (RBMS). Standards Committee (1983). Genre Terms: a Thesaurus for use in rare book and special collections cataloguing. *College and Research Libraries News*, 9, pp. 322-25. (2nd ed. expected 1991).

———— (1988a). *Binding Terms: A Thesaurus for Use in Rare Book and Special Collections Cataloguing*. Chicago, IL: ALA/ACRL.

———— (1988b). *Provenance Evidence: A Thesaurus for Use in Rare Book and Special Collections Cataloguing*. Chicago, IL: ALA/ACRL.

Attig, J. (1983). The Concept of a MARC format. *Information Technology and Libraries*, 2, pp. 7-17.

Becker, P. (1987). Möglichkeiten der Standardisierung bei Metaquellen. F. Haus-mann, R. Hartell, I. H. Krópac, & P. Becker (Eds.), *Data Networks for the Historical Disciplines: Problems and Feasibilities in Standardization and Exchange of Machine Readable Data* (pp. 18-27). Graz: Leykam.

Beit-Arie, M. (1981). *Hebrew Codicology: Tentative Typology of Technical Terms Employed in Hebrew Medieval Manuscripts*.

Bourlet, C., Doutrelepont, C. and Lusignan S. (1982). *Ordinateur et études mediévales: Bibliographie*. Montréal: Institut d'études médiévales.

Bourlet, C. and Minel, J.-L. (1989). An Expert Decision Support System for a Prosopographical Database. L. J. McCrank (Ed.), *Data Bases in the Humanities and Social Sciences*, 4 (pp. 79-84). Medford, N.J.: Learned Information.

Brately, P. and Hamesse, J. (1990). The Computerisation of Manuscript Incipits. In Hamesse, J., Zampoli, A., Choueka, Y. (Eds.), *Computers in Literary and Linguistic Research*, Proceedings of the Fifteenth International Conference on Literary and Linguistic Computing, Jerusalem, 5-9 June 1988. Paris-Geneva: Champion-Slatkine.

Brown, M. P. (1990). *A Guide to Western Historical Scripts*. Toronto: University of Toronto Press.

Brown, T. Julian (1959-63). Latin Paleography since Traube. *Transactions of the Cambridge Bibliographic Society*, 3, pp. 361-81.

———— (1974). Paleography. *New Cambridge Bibliography of English Literature* (vols. 20-21). Cambridge University Press.

Chen, C. (1989). Large-scale multi-media database in the Humanities: a case presentation of PROJECT EMPEROR I. L. J. McCrank (Ed.), *Data Bases in the Humanities and Social Sciences, 1987* (pp. 139-149). Medford, N.J.: Learned Information.

Corbett, J. A. (1978). *Catalogue of the Medieval and Renaissance Manuscripts of the University of Notre Dame*. South Bend, Indiana: Association of the University of Notre Dame Library.

Courthouts, J. (1987). A MARC-format for medieval codices. In *Gazxette du livre médiéval 11*, 13-17.

Delaissé, L. M. J. (1967). Toward a History of the Medieval Book. *Miscellanea Andres Combs*, v. 2; repr., *Divinitas, 11*, pp. 423-35.

Delaissé, L. M. J., Parkes, M. and Marrow, J. (1977). *Illuminated Manuscripts: The James A. de Rothschild Collection at Waddeston Manor*. Fribourg, Switzerland: National Trust.

Denley, P. & Hopkin, P. (1990). *History and Computing*. Manchester: University of Manchester Press.

Derolez, A. (1973). Codicologie ou Archeologie du Livre. *Scriptorium, 27*: 47-49.

Dutschke, C. W., *et alii*. (1989). *Guide to Medieval and Renaissance Manuscripts in the Huntington Library*. San Marino, CA: Huntington Library.

Etherington, D. and Roberts, R. (1982). *Bookbinding and the Conservation of Books: A Dictionary of Descriptive Terminology*. Washington, D.C.

Faulhaber, C. (1983). *Medieval Manuscripts in the Library of the Hispanic Society in America . . .* (2 vols.). New York: Hispanic Society of America.

Geuenich, D. (1988). A database for research on names and groups of persons in the middle ages. *Data Base Oriented Source Editions: Papers from . . . 23rd International Congress on Medieval Studies* (pp. 9-14). Kalamazoo, Michigan.

Gruijs, A. (1972). Codicology or Archeology of the Books? — a false dilemma. *Querendo, 2*: 87-108.

Hahn, N. L. (1990). The Future of Computerized Manuscript Catalogues. A Proposal. Eds. Folkerts, M. and Kühne, A. *The Use of Computers in Cataloging Medieval and Renaissance Manuscripts*. Algorismus 4 (pp. 41-56). Munich: Institut für Geschichte der Naturwissenschaften.

———— (1991). Three Steps from Typewriter to Catalogue (pp. 10-45).

Hahn, N. L., Stevens, W. M. and Sorenson, B. L. (1983). *The Benjamin Data Bank and BAG/2: A Case Study and User Manual for Encoding, Storing, and Retrieving Information on Medieval Manuscripts*. Dunellen, N.J.: Benjamin Data Bank.

Hamesse, J. (1990). Automated Retrieval of Incipits for Access to Manuscripts. Paper at the International Congress of Historical Sciences, Madrid, Aug. 29-Sept. 3, 1990.

Härtel, H. *et alii* (Eds.) (1986). Probleme des Bearbeitung mittelalterlicher Handschriften. *Wolfenbütteler Forschungen, 30*. Wiesbaden: O. Harrassowitz.

Hausmann, F., Hartel R., Krópac, H. I., and Becker, P. (Eds.) (1987). *Data Networks for the Historical Disciplines: Problems and Feasibilities in Standardization and Exchange of Machine-Readable Data*. Graz: Leykam.

Hensen, S. L. (1989). *Archives, Personal Papers and Manuscripts: A Cataloging Manual for Archival Repositories, Historical Societies, and Manuscript Libraries* (2nd ed.). Chicago: Society of American Archivists. 1st ed., 1983.

Hersberg, T. (1973). *The Philadelphia Social History Project. A Methodological History*. MA thesis: Stanford University.

———— (1981). Archival Automation and the Researcher. L. J. McCrank (Ed.), *Automating the Archives: Issues and Problems in Computer Applications* (pp. 35-66). White Plains, N.Y.: Knowledge Industry Publications, for ASIS.

Hume, L. P. (1989). The Research Libraries Group's Research Information Management Program: New information resources for scholars. L. J. McCrank (Ed.), *Data Bases in the Humanities and Social Sciences, 4* (pp. 343-346). Medford, N.J.: Learned Information.

IFLA. Committee on Cataloging (1975). *List of Uniform Titles for Liturgical Works in the Latin Rites of the Catholic Church*. London: IFLA.

Krópac, I. H. (1989). The Prosopographical data bank for the history of the southeast territories of the old "Reich" to 1250. L. J. McCrank (Ed.), *Data Bases in the Humanities and Social Sciences, 4* (pp. 383-390). Medford, N.J.: Learned Information.

Krópac, I. H. and Becker, P. (1989). Die prosopographische Datenbank zur Geschichte der sudostlichen Reichsgebeite bis 1250. Konzepte und Kurzdokumentation. *Medium Aevum Quotidianum, 10*, pp. 40-65.

Leonhard, J.-F. (Ed.) (1985). *Methoden und Probleme der Katalogisierung Abbendaendischer Handschriften. Die Tagung der Handschriftenbearbeiter in Wolfenbüttel vom 24. bis 26. 8. 1984* in *Zeitschrift für Bibliothekwesen und Bibliographie, 32* (5).

Library of Congress (1981). *Bibliographic Description of Rare Books: Rules Formulated Under AACR2 and ISBD(A) for the Descriptive Cataloging of Rare Books and Other Special Printed Materials*. Washington, D.C.: Library of Congress Descriptive Cataloging. Current revision expected in 1991.

Lytle, R. (1984). An Analysis of the work of the National Information Systems Task Force. *American Archivist, 47*, pp. 357-365.

McCrank, L. J. (1979). Analytical and Historical Bibliography: A State of the Art Review (pp. 175-85). D. Carbonneau (Ed.), *Annual Report of the American Rare, Antiquarian and Out-of-Print Book Trade, 1978/1979*. New York, New York: BCAR Publications.

———— (1980). *Education for Rare Book Librarianship: A Re-examination of Trends and Problems*. In *Occasional Papers, 144*. Urbana, Illinois: University of Illinois Graduate School of Library Science.

———— (1981). *Automating the Archives: Issues and Problems in Computer Applications*. White Plains, New York: Knowledge Industry Publications, for ASIS.

———— (1983a). The Mt. Angel Rare Book and Manuscript Cataloging Project.

S. Burton & D. Short (Eds.), *Sixth International Conference on Computers and the Humanities* (pp. 414-430). Washington, D.C.: Computer Science Press.

———— (1983b). *The Rare Book and Manuscript Collections of Mt. Angel Abbey Library: A Catalog and Index* (461 pp., 5-fiche program). Wilmington, Del.: Scholarly Resources.

———— (1984). Rare Book Cataloging: Improved Standards and Rising Costs. *Cataloging and Classification Quarterly, 5* (1), pp. 27-51.

———— (1985). Strategic Planning for Networking of Rare Books and Historical Manuscript Data Resources. R. F. Allen (Ed.), *International Conference on Data Bases in the Humanities and Social Sciences* (pp. 193-208). Osprey, Florida: Paradigm Press; now available from Learned Information, Medford, New Jersey.

———— (1986a). The Impact of Automation: Integrating Archival and Bibliographic Systems. *Journal of Library Administration*, 7, pp. 61-97.

———— (1986b). Medieval Libraries. J. Strayer (Ed.), *Dictionary of the Middle Ages* (vol. 7, pp. 557-570). New York: C. Scribners for the American Council of Learned Societies.

———— (1987). Linking Bibliography and Archival Information Systems: Indexing Terms and Stratified Vocabularies. H. Czap & C. Galinski (Eds.), *Terminology and Knowledge Engineering: Proceedings of the International Conference on Terminological Sciences, Trier, 1987* (vol. 2, pp. 128-132). Frankfurt am Main: Index Verlag.

———— (Ed.) (1988). *Data Bases in the Humanities and Social Sciences, 1987* (vol. 4). Medford, New Jersey: Learned Information.

———— (1989). Sharing Codicological Resources through Networks. H. Veder (Ed.), *International Data Bases for Medieval Manuscript Studies* (Katholieke Universiteit, Nijmegen), in *Polata Knigopisnaja, 17-18*, pp. 30-59.

———— (1990). Archival and Museum Informatics: A Review Essay. *Special Collections, 4* (2), pp. 117-132.

———— [1991a in press]. Medieval Libraries (30 pp.). W. Wiegand & D. Davis (Eds.), *Encyclopedia of Library History*. New York: Greenwood Press.

———— [1991b forthcoming]. Paradigms and Decision Support Systems for Reference Expertise. *Reference Services*.

McCrank, L. J. and Batty, C. D. (1978). Cataloging with FAMULUS: The Manuscripts and Rare Book Collection of Mt. Angel Abbey. *Computers and Humanities, 12*, pp. 215-222.

McCrank, L. J. and Elvove, J. (1983). The Mt. Angel Abbey Rare Book and Manuscript Project Revisited: A Case Study in Automated Cataloguing and Publishing. In *Proceedings: Sixth International Conference on Computers and the Humanities* (pp. 415-430). Washington, D.C.: Computer Science Press.

Muzerelle, D. (1985). *Vocabulaire Codicologique: repertoire methodique des termes francais relatifs aux manuscrits*. Paris: Eds. CEMI.

Needham, P. (1979). *Five Centuries of Bookbinding, 400-1600*. New York & London: Pierpont Morgan Library & Oxford University Press.

Oikawa, A. (1989). Archeological Image Database System. L. J. McCrank (Ed.), *Data Bases in the Humanities and Social Sciences, 4* (pp. 501-507). Medford, NJ: Learned Information.

Parkes, M. (1979). *The Medieval Manuscripts of Keble College.* Oxford University Press.

Riggs, D., Aluri, R. (Eds.) (1990). *Expert Systems in Libraries.* Norwood, New Jersey: Ablex Pub. Corp.

Saenger, P. (1989). *A Catalogue of the Pre-1500 Western Manuscript Books at the Newberry Library.* Chicago, Illinois: University of Chicago Press.

Sahli, N. (1985). *MARC for Archives and Manuscripts: The AMC Format.* Chicago: Society of American Archivists.

Sanjian, A. K. (1976). *A Catalog of Medieval Armenian Manuscripts in the United States.* Berkeley, California: University of California Press.

Schutzner, S. (1989). *Medieval and Renaissance Manuscript Books in the Library of Congress: A Description Catalog* (vol. 1 to date: *Bible, Liturgy, Books of Hours*). Washington, D.C.: Library of Congress.

Schurer, K. (1990). Artificial intelligence and the historian—prospects and possibilities. R. Ennals & J. C. Gardin (Eds.), *Interpretation in the Humanities* (pp. 169-95). London: British Library.

Shailor, B. A. (1984). *Catalogue of Medieval and Renaissance Manuscripts in the Beinecke Rare Room and Manuscript Library of Yale University.* Binghamton, New York: Medieval & Renaissance Texts and Studies.

Smets, J. (1990). *Creer une base de donnees historiques avec KLEIO.* Gottingen: Max-Planck-Institut für Geschichte.

Snyder, H. (1979). ESTC: A Progress Report (pp. 162-5). D. Carboneau (Ed.), *Annual Report of the American Rare, Antiquarian, and Out-of-Print Book Trade.* New York: BCAR Publications.

Stalker, D. (1991). A Comparison of Catalog Entries in *ESTC* and Bibliographic Descriptions in D. F. Foxon's *English Verse, 1701-1756. Special Collections, 4* (2), pp. 9-38.

Tanselle, G. T. (1974a). The bibliographic description of paper. *Studies in Bibliography, 24,* pp. 27-67.

——— (1974b). Bibliography as a Science. *Studies in Bibliography, 27,* pp. 55-89.

——— (1979). The State of Bibliography Today. *Papers of the Bibliographical Society of America, 73,* pp. 289-304.

Thaller, M. (1987). *KLEIO. A Data Base System for Historical Research. Version 1.1.1.* Göttingen: Max-Planck Institut für Geschichte.

Thomas, J. B. III (1987). The Necessity of Standards in an Automated Environment. M. V. Cloonan (Ed.), *Recent Trends in Rare Book Librarianship,* in *Library Trends, 36* (1), pp. 125-139.

Turner, E.G., (1968). *Greek papyri, An Introduction.* Oxford University Press.

Van der Horst, K., (1990). *Illuminated and Decorated Medieval Manuscripts in the University Library, Utrecht. An Illustrated Catalog.* Cambridge University Press.

Van Wingen, P. and Douglas, S. P. (1982). *Standard Citation Forms for Published Bibliographies and Catalogs Used in Rare Book Cataloging.* Washington, D.C.: Library of Congress.

Wellish, H. (1975). *The Conversion of Scripts: Its Nature, History, and Utilization.* (Rev. ed., 1978). New York: Wiley.

Weijers, O. (Ed.) (1989). *Vocabulaire du livre et de l'ecriture au moyen âge.* Turnhout.

Wilson, W. J. (1956). Manuscript Cataloging. *Traditio, 12,* 456-555.

Winter, U., Schipke, R. and Teitge, H.-E. (1983). *Regeln für die Katalogisierung von Handschriften [im Auftrage der Deutschen Staatsbibliothek . . .].* Berlin: Deutsche Staatsbibliothek, Kommission für Handschriften und Inkunabeln.

Manuscript Census Record

Thomas L. Amos

SUMMARY. A practical step for libraries and research scholars alike would be to separate two levels of data concerning the cataloguing of primary sources in manuscript. The great number of details usually provided by current standards of manuscript descriptions may be too great for MARC to handle. But there is a first level of data in any catalogue description of a manuscript which corresponds very well with the data for printed books in MARC-based catalogues. Amos therefore proposed a First-Level-Record to be provided for any and every manuscript in a library book catalogue. It could be created and exchanged easily in MARC format. This is called the Manuscript Census Record.

Description of medieval and renaissance manuscript books (codices manuscripti) can be obtained at present mainly from printed catalogues or locally available card-catalogues. Both sources are often difficult to locate. Often such information is available only at the library or archive holding the original document in question. When manuscript descriptions can be found, they exist in a variety of formats, each of which differs from formats employed elsewhere. Recently numerous attempts have been made to create computer-assisted manuscript catalogues which would offer the researcher the possibility of on-line access to manuscript descriptions. To date, however, only one such system, MEDIUM created by the Institut de Recherche et d'Histoire des Textes in Paris, offers the opportunity to access a fairy full range of information about manuscripts through use of a modem.

To improve this situation and to promote a standard form of computer-based manuscript census record, the International Committee

Professor Thomas L. Amos is Lecturer in History at Saint John's University and Rare Book Librarian in the Alcuin Library. He is the author of several volumes of a new catalogue of manuscripts of the Fundo Alcobaça, Biblioteca Nacional, Lisbon, and has published several studies of Carolingian sermons.

for the Establishment of a Machine-Readable Manuscript Census Record (MCR) has been formed under the chairmanship of Professor Wesley Stevens of the University of Winnipeg. Membership of the Committee reflects current projects involving computer cataloguing of manuscripts from a variety of European and North American institutions. The Committee proposes that a standard machine-readable census level record for manuscript descriptions be based on the First-Level Record suggested by Amos in a paper presented to the International Workshop on the Use of Computers in Manuscript Cataloguing at the Deutsches Museum, Munich, August 10-12, 1989. The type of record we propose could be used by manuscript libraries and archives, microfilm manuscript libraries and collections holding manuscript descriptions to provide researchers with information, accessible by computer, about their holdings.

PROPOSED MCR STANDARD

A First-Level Record is not a complete codicological or contents-based description of an individual manuscript and its contents. Yet we believe that it provides sufficient information to enable a researcher to determine whether or not a manuscript would be of use for a particular piece of research work. The record proposed by MCR contains the following fields:

STRUCTURE OF A FIRST-LEVEL RECORD

Institution   Country
City   Library   Shelfmark
Project Number   Folia/Pages Date
Further Computer Description Available [Y/N]
Beginning and Ending Foliation
Author   Title   Incipit
Typology   Typology Name
Language
(Repeated as necessary for each item)
Published Description: [Y/N]
Source of Information   [C/M/D]

EXPLANATIONS

Institution: Identity of the institution supplying the description; may be different from City and Library fields below.

Country; City; Library: Present location of original document.

Shelfmark: Precise classification and identifying label of the document, includes former shelfmarks, if any, as olim and numbers.

Project Number: Holding Institution's classifying and identifying number if different from shelfmark (microfilm shelfmark or call number).

Folia/Pages: Supplied in Roman numerals for endleaves and Arabic numerals for folia/pages of main text.

Complete or Partial: Indicates nature of holding for microfilm libraries.

Date: Century or year(s) in which manuscript was written, supplied in Arabic numerals, i.e., 13c (1278).

Further Computer Description Available: Yes or no, in reference to a computer-based record held by the institution furnishing the First-Level record.

Beginning and Ending Foliation: for individual works within each manuscript.

Author: Use standard forms where they exist for works to 1500.

Title: Use standard forms where they exist for works to 1500.

Incipit: Given in form Pericope (Book Chapter: Verse); [Prologue] or [Prologue 1] [Prologue 2] . . . and [Text].

Typology: Nature of work: original work; translation; or commentary.

Typology Name: Translator or author of commentary.

Language: Language(s) of work.

Published Description: For the entire manuscript, i.e., printed catalogues or specialized studies as Yes or No.

Source of Information: Does this record describe, and use as a source of information, an original document (C); microform (M); description (D) or some combination of the three.

The First-Level Record, as should be evident from this description, is not intended to replace full descriptions. Nor is it intended to replace the development of full-description computer-based catalogues. Instead, it provides a means to establish from existing computer-based or printed information a series of local, regional, national or even international on-line computer manuscript censuses which will help researchers to be better able to locate important primary sources. The metaphor employed here is simple but important. A First-Level record is a census or "card-catalogue" record. At the second level lies the fuller computer-based or printed description of the manuscript or microfilmed manuscript, where these exist. Finally, at the third level, there remains the examination of the document or microform itself. The First-Level record is only a guide to the remaining levels of information. Its true significance lies in its potential for use as a vehicle for the collection, storage and retrieval of large numbers of such records. In time, we hope that the MCR standard will lead to the creation of and International On-Line Union Catalogue of manuscript holdings throughout the world.

GOALS

The work of the Committee will be undertaken under seven broad headings:

- Establishment of a standard MCR record.
- Consulting with the proper authorities to establish liaison between the MCR standard and current printed-book library records for manuscript books.
- Creation of a data storage and retrieval structure for MCR records.
- Establishing agreement on a set of standard author and title forms.
- Gaining the agreement of individual institutions to contribute MCR records for their holdings.
- Securing the establishment of Central Registers of MCR records at the national, regional and international levels.
- Overseeing maintenance of the MCR standard and access to the data.

While the Committee has undertaken the work of establishing the MCR standard, we shall be seeking the advice and suggestions of scholars, manuscript cataloguers and librarians concerning possible revisions in format and other matters.

CONTRIBUTING MEMBERS

We ask that Contributing Members accept the MCR record structure, and undertake to supply as quickly as possible the requisite information for all fields of the record structure that they can. Information should be submitted as ASCII text on an IBM-DOS or MS-DOS formatted floppy disk(s). The ASCII data received will be loaded into the storage and retrieval system at one of the Central Registers. On its part, the Committee will undertake to supply each Contributing Member with a copy of the data storage and retrieval structure and instructions on its use for the local benefit of each contributing institution.

Where information for one or more of the MCR fields is not presently available, such as Date or Incipit, we ask that the Contributing Member agree to supply such information within a mutually agreed-upon reasonable period of time, or to make such arrangements as are necessary with the Committee to insure that the missing information can eventually be supplied.

INTERNATIONAL COMMITTEE
FOR THE MANUSCRIPT CENSUS RECORD

Professor Wesley Stevens
Chairman, MCR
Department of History
University of Winnipeg
515 Portage Avenue
Winnipeg, Manitoba R3B 2E9

Prof. Dr. Menso Folkerts
Institut für Geschichte
der Naturwissenschaften
Museuminsel 1
8000 Munich 26

Dr. Thomas Amos
Secretary, MCR
Alcuin Library
Saint John's University
Collegeville, MN 56321

Dr. Hope Mayo
Pierpont Morgan Library
29 East 36th Street
New York, NY 10016

Dr. Andreas Kühne
Institut für Geschichte
der Naturwissenschaften
Museuminsel 1
8000 Munich 26

Mme. Agnès Guillaumont
Institut de Recherche et
d'Histoire des Textes
40 Avenue d'Iena
75116 Paris

Author Index

Names of ancient and modern authors are cited from each text and its footnotes, but not those names mentioned only in abstracts, author identifications, references and citations, or appendices. The author index was prepared by W. M. Stevens and M. Bielewicz, University of Winnipeg.

187

Subject Index

References are to the terms used in each text and its footnotes, but not to terms used in abstracts, author identifications, references and citations, or appendices. Field list items used by these cataloguing systems are also not indexed in detail. The index was prepared by W. M. Stevens and M. Bielewicz.